THE SOILING OF OLD GLORY

Autumn Glory: Baseball's First World Series

1831: Year of Eclipse

*Rites of Execution: Capital Punishment and the
Transformation of American Culture, 1776–1865*

THE SOILING
OF OLD GLORY

THE STORY OF A PHOTOGRAPH
THAT SHOCKED AMERICA

LOUIS P. MASUR

BLOOMSBURY PRESS

Published by Bloomsbury Press, New York
Distributed to the trade by Holtzbrinck Publishers

All papers used by Bloomsbury Press are natural, recyclable products made from wood grown in well-managed forests. The manufacturing processes conform to the environmental regulations of the country of origin.

LIBRARY OF CONGRESS CATALOGING-IN-PUBLICATION DATA

Masur, Louis P.
The soiling of Old Glory : the story of a photograph that shocked America / Louis P. Masur. — 1st U.S. ed.
p. cm.
Includes bibliographical references and index.
ISBN-13: 978-1-59691-364-6 (alk. paper)
ISBN-10: 1-59691-364-9 (alk. paper)
1. Boston (Mass.)—Race relations—History—20th century.   2. Flags—Desecration—United States—Pictorial works.   3. Photojournalism—Social aspects—United States—Case studies.   4. Photojournalism—Political aspects—United States—Case studies.   5. Protest movements—Massachusetts—Boston—History—20th century.   6. Busing for school integration—Massachusetts—Boston—History—20th century.   7. African Americans—Massachusetts—Boston—Interviews.   8. Whites—Massachusetts—Boston—Interviews.   9. Interviews—Massachusetts—Boston.   10. United States—Race relations—History—20th century.   I. Title.

F73.9.A1M38 2008
974.4'6100496073—dc22
2007031215

"America," from *Collected Poems 1947–1980* by Allen Ginsberg. Copyright © 1956, 1959 by Allen Ginsberg. Reprinted by permission of HarperCollins Publishers.

"Thunder Road" by Bruce Springsteen. Copyright © 1975 Bruce Springsteen, renewed © 2003 Bruce Springsteen (ASCAP). Reprinted by permission. International copyright secured. All rights reserved.

First U.S. Edition 2008

1 3 5 7 9 10 8 6 4 2

Typeset by Westchester Book Group
Printed in the United States of America by Quebecor World Fairfield

For Tom, Doug, and Jim
and to the memory of my parents

CONTENTS

PREFACE

THE TEENAGER SAT on the subway, daydreaming in the late afternoon as he rode to his part-time job cleaning offices in downtown Boston. He looked up and saw a man across the aisle holding open the *Herald American*, one of the city's two newspapers. Front-page center was a staggering photograph of an angry white protester thrusting an American flag at a black man whose arms are being held. He wondered: who is that lunatic with the flag? In the same instant he realized that it was him. He skipped work and went home to South Boston. "I think I have a problem," he told his parents.

Nearly thirty years later, in 2005, residents across Boston held a series of City-Wide Dialogues on Boston's Ethnic and Racial Diversity. To one meeting, someone brought Stanley Forman's Pulitzer Prize–winning photograph that had appeared on April 6, 1976, in the *Herald American*, and in newspapers across the country. The participants at the meeting had been quiet, but the image of a black man being assaulted with the American flag broke the silence. Michael James, a thirty-nine-year-old African American resident of Roxbury, said, "Everybody in the room no matter their race was appalled. It accelerated the conversation. It was like: 'We do have something in common. We don't want this to ever happen again.'"

Stanley Forman, The Soiling of Old Glory, *1976* (COURTESY STANLEY FORMAN, SJFORMAN@VERIZON.NET)

The photograph presents a sickening sight. A well-dressed black man is being grabbed from behind. He seems to be struggling to free himself. His satchel lies behind him at his feet. A large crowd, composed mostly of high school students, looks on. The flag bearer's feet are planted, his hands firmly grasping the staff, his eyes focused on his target. His hair flows back as he prepares to lunge forward. Attacker and victim are forever frozen in time, and we feel trapped beside them. We can glance away, but we cannot escape the horror of what we imagine the next instant will bring.

Forman's photograph, taken on April 5, 1976, is implanted in the collective memory and identity of Boston and the nation. One commentator called it "the shot heard round the world for its indelible portrait of American racism." In the more than thirty years since the picture was taken, the image has often been invoked, especially when an event has some racial dimension. In the Massachusetts election for governor in 2006, the possibility that Deval Patrick would become the first African American elected statewide since Senator Edward Brooke more than three decades earlier brought repeated references to the image. After Patrick was chosen the first black governor in the state's history, an op-ed in the *Boston Globe* began with reference to the photograph—"one of the most notorious icons in Massachusetts history . . . It was an ugly moment and an unforgettable picture—and all the proof countless viewers needed that Boston was a caldron of bigotry." The writer hoped that "Patrick's inauguration will finally wash away the shameful stain of that day in 1976."

Boston is not the only city that has been defined by a harrowing image of racial hatred, but Forman's photograph is distinctive. Many of the most notorious images of racial violence involve police brutality—the authorities using excessive force against African Americans. Think of police dogs set loose upon civil rights marchers in Birmingham or the beating of Rodney King in Los Angeles. In contrast, Forman's shot captures one citizen attacking another. And it was not just any violent assault, but one that employed the American flag as a weapon—in the year of the nation's Bicentennial, no less. It was an unprecedented act of desecration, one that transgressed every principle most Americans held dear.

The image, taken eighteen months into the battle over the desegregation of the public schools, crystallized Boston's reputation as a racist city. For more than a generation, the city has struggled to overcome the damage done by the busing crisis, for which Forman's photograph, rightly or wrongly, is taken as the defining moment. The picture punctured the nation's comfortable illusion that the struggle over civil rights was primarily a southern phenomenon. Even the pictures from Little Rock in 1957, of screaming white women stalking a young black student on her way to school, pale in comparison to the hatred captured here. An assault against a black man with the American flag in Boston, the so-called Cradle of Liberty, made the image all the more revolting.

Not only in Boston but also across the nation the photograph served as a harsh reminder that the triumphs of the civil rights movement of the 1950s and 1960s had turned tragic. Progress had been made, but alongside it stood backlash and failure. Americans cherished stories of wrongs righted, of darkness yielding to light, but Forman's picture provided a poisonous counter-narrative. The brotherhood of man was a worthy ideal, and it even seemed at times that a strong foundation had been laid for its realization. But in a claustrophobic courtyard, a white man turned the American flag against a black man, and the ideal crumbled.

I cannot recall when I first saw the photograph. It is possible I saw it in the *New York Times* when I was a college student. I certainly saw it reproduced in various histories of civil rights I read in graduate school. I remember staring at the image for long stretches of time, and wondering about the story. Who did this? What happened? Why is the photograph so compelling? Few works talked in any detail about the picture, and the captions said little. Books used it as an illustration, its meaning supposedly self-evident. But the picture not only recorded something awful, it also shaped what followed. It is an image that is felt as much as seen, a searing image that discomfits yet demands our attention. The photograph stayed with me over the years, as it has with many who saw it in 1976 or since.

A few years ago, I contacted Stanley Forman. I met with him, and he told me the story of the shot, shared with me the other pictures he took that day, and talked about his career. As I researched the image, I learned the identities of some of the individuals in the photograph. I watched a video of the press conference held two days after the incident by the man who was attacked. And I read Thomas Farragher's remarkable two-part piece about the flag bearer and the victim that appeared in the *Boston Globe* on the twenty-fifth anniversary of the event in 2001.

Accepting the suggestion of an editor, Bill Lewis at the *Herald American*, Forman titled the picture *The Soiling of Old Glory* when he submitted it in 1976 for Pulitzer Prize consideration. It is a title that complements the photograph perfectly. Using "Old Glory" rather than simply "the flag" tied the photograph to the deepest struggles of the nation's history. The verb *soiling* means defiling or staining. But with the root *soil*, it also suggests planting. Flags are thrust into the ground as statements of control, whether by explorers in the New World or American astronauts on the moon. In an extreme act of desecration and possession, the protester, it seems, is trying to implant the flag into the black man and claim ownership.

WHAT FOLLOWS IS the story of the photograph. An examination of the making and meaning of a single image entails narrating the incident, reading the photograph, analyzing its immediate impact, and assessing its effect on the lives of some of the people involved. It also requires a survey of the history of the controversy over busing and the story of the veneration and desecration of the flag, topics that provide essential contexts for fully understanding the image.

Photographs do not speak for themselves. Like all texts, they must be read. Ours may be a visual culture, but we are not necessarily visually literate. Look closely at any photograph. What do we see? How do we unpack it? Why does it move us? Every image evokes other images, and the connections add depth to our understanding. Photographs simultaneously document and interpret events. They hold us in their spell by freezing action, and those frozen, decisive moments reveal and conceal, show what is and what may not actually be. A reading of *The Soiling of Old Glory* carries with it surprises about what happened on that April day.

In an instant (1/250th of a second), Forman's photograph sealed Boston's reputation as a racist city and shattered the illusion that the country had made progress in race relations. For more than thirty years, Americans have had to confront the image's implications. It turns out that among those who have worked hardest to reverse Boston's fortunes is the battered man in the center of Forman's frame. A biography of *The Soiling of Old Glory* is the story of a wrenching image, its impact, and how a city, and the nation, have come to redefine themselves, not by trying to efface a photograph from historical memory, but by pondering and transforming its meaning.

CHAPTER 1

THE INCIDENT

THE DAY BROKE mild and clear. Early April in Boston could bring slicing winds and numbing cold, but on Monday morning, April 5, spring had staked its claim. Students in South Boston and Charlestown, never ones to overdress even in the depths of winter, ventured out in light jackets and windbreakers, and some even in shirtsleeves. The previous Friday, fliers had appeared all over the high schools calling for a Monday boycott of classes to rally against busing at City Hall Plaza and the Federal Building. This had become a familiar drill for many of the teens. Ever since U.S. District Judge Arthur Garrity had ruled in June 1974 that Boston had deliberately maintained segregated schools, and ordered a program of busing to promote desegregation, boycotts, protests, and violence had afflicted the schools and the city.

Some two hundred white students assembled for the march to City Hall Plaza. They attended for every reason, and for no reason at all: they despised forced busing, they hated blacks, they feared change, they followed their parents' lead, they welcomed days off from school, they wanted to hang out with their friends, they felt like they were part of a group. "We all wanted to belong to something big," recalls one teenage protester, "and the feeling of being part of the anti-busing movement along with the rest of Southie had been the best feeling in the world." Southie meant more than just the geographic place South Boston. It meant neighborhood and community and ethnic pride. Thinking of the long day ahead, some packed a snack. Some made signs that said RESIST. One student, Joseph Rakes, before leaving his third-floor South Boston apartment, grabbed the family's American flag.

From the start, the anti-busing movement identified itself with patriotism. The activists saw themselves as defending their liberty against the tyranny of a judge run amok. The celebration of Bicentennial events in 1975 and 1976 only reinforced the idea that they were carrying on in a tradition of American resistance; one anti-busing group had as its motto "Don't tread on me." At rallies and boycotts, protesters carried American flags and frequently sang "God Bless America." Protesters against the Vietnam War had often burned Old Glory, but not here, not among the mainly working-class Irish of Boston.

Some adults accompanied the students on the march. Part organizers, part chaperones, they kept the group moving and looked to help avoid any trouble. One of the leaders was James Kelly, a South Boston spokesman since the conflict began and president of the South Boston Information Center. Kelly had graduated in 1958 from South Boston High School, where he played football and learned a trade. He became a sheet metal worker, putting in long hours and raising a family in South Boston. Kelly was a working-class kid. "My father didn't make much money," he said. "We were renters all our lives. I understand what it's like to live week to week."

Kelly lost his way on the path to economic stability in 1967 when he was convicted of possessing a dangerous weapon. He spent four months at the Suffolk County House of Correction and emerged with a record. His drinking problem, which helped land him in jail in the first place, worsened: "My weekends began on Thursday and ended on Tuesday. I started to realize I wasn't a very nice guy to my family." With the help of his parole officer and Alcoholics Anonymous, Kelly got sober. He recalls having had his last drink on March 24, 1971. Then he started to turn his life around.

In 1973, Kelly suffered an injury on his job—sheet metal sliced the tendons in his right hand—and he received workman's compensation. At that moment, the busing crisis took hold of him. He and City Council president Louise Day Hicks, whose actions on the Boston School Committee in the 1960s led to the lawsuit that resulted in the desegregation order, were neighbors and friends, so even though Kelly himself did not get involved in politics, he supported the efforts to defend his community against busing and charges of racism. With Garrity's decision, Kelly became active. Through the South Boston Information Center, organized in early September 1974 to offset negative and inaccurate press reports about opposition to busing, he helped direct resistance. Kelly organized the protest on April 5.

When the marchers arrived at City Hall, Louise Day Hicks invited them into the empty council chamber. Hicks embodied the South Boston community. Her father, a distinguished lawyer and banker, was also a special justice on the South Boston District Court. After he died, she devoted herself to education, the law, and politics. She earned a bachelor's degree at age thirty-six and a law degree three years later. Elected to the School Committee in 1961, she soon found herself at the center of a debate over de facto segregation in the schools. She lost a close election for mayor in 1967. She served on the City Council and one term as a congresswoman. Hicks was now the leader of the council. When Judge Garrity issued his order, she helped found ROAR—Restore Our Alienated Rights, an organization militantly opposed to busing. For months, she kept a ROAR poster in her office, high above City Hall Plaza.

Hicks had not known that the students were coming until she heard it announced on the radio. She looked out of her office window onto the plaza and saw them walking, carrying signs. A few went to her office. The students presented a list of their demands: they wanted an end to busing, they wanted accurate reporting of racial incidents, and they wanted the superintendent to resign. Hicks, who often wore hats and gloves and bright-colored dresses and projected a ladylike manner that seemed at odds with the anger that engulfed her, served hot chocolate to the marchers, and together in the council chamber everyone said the Pledge of Allegiance. The students stood proudly. One held an American flag in his left hand and placed his right hand over his heart. Hicks herself often wore a rhinestone-spangled flag pin and had once declared that "the flag is motherhood and apple pie."

As the students filed out of the chamber and headed outside, they passed a group of black students from a nearby magnet school going on a tour. Some epithets were exchanged, and pieces of food—donuts, cookies, apples—flew back and forth. Groups have moods, and the protesters, fueled with cocoa and patriotism, marched onto the plaza feeling righteous about their cause. At that moment, a black man turned the corner and headed in their direction.

Ted Landsmark was late to a meeting. A lawyer for the Contractors Association, he was headed to City Hall for discussions on minority hiring in construction jobs. Dressed well on this mild April morning in a favorite three-piece suit, he was enjoying the brisk walk.

Pledge of Allegiance, *1976* (*BOSTON HERALD AMERICAN*)

This was only Landsmark's third year in Boston. Born Theodore Augustus Burrell in Kansas City in 1946, he grew up in public housing in East Harlem after his family came east to be with relatives. His father worked as a subway conductor; his mother was a nurse. His parents separated when he was three, and Landsmark was raised by his doting mother as well as his grandparents and two aunts. When he moved to Boston, he took his mother's maiden name, to "honor the woman who did all the work."

Landsmark's dawning political consciousness came from his grandfather, who was a follower of Marcus Garvey, the black nationalist leader and founder of the Universal Negro Improvement Association. The young Landsmark watched his grandfather come home from the coal yards and wash up with grit to get the grime off of his hands. Then he would settle down with a Ballantine Ale and a copy of the *New York Times* and preach to whoever was listening about the events of the day.

Childhood polio left Landsmark with a slight limp and unable to participate as fully in sports as he would have liked. At New York's elite Stuyvesant High School he found an outlet for his athletic interests and at the same time learned some important lessons about organizing.

Landsmark joined the cheerleading squad, in part to meet girls. He also learned that, as captain of the cheerleaders, he could lead in any direction he pleased. He started mobilizing students for events away from Stuyvesant. He invited them to the March on Washington in 1963, which he attended with his grandparents and aunts. He led his classmates to Union Square to see President Kennedy's motorcade. And he organized a rally to protest a speech by George Lincoln Rockwell of the American Nazi Party. He had little difficulty getting the many Jewish students at Stuyvesant to skip school for that one.

After a year at St. Paul's in New Hampshire, where he was in the first cohort of blacks ever to attend the prep school, Landsmark went to Yale in 1964. He was one of sixteen black students in the freshman class, and it did not take long for him to become central to the civil rights movement both on campus and off. He served as political editor for the *Yale Daily News*, got interested in photojournalism, and had his first experiences in the Deep South when he answered an ad placed by some divinity students looking for help driving down to support the freedom marches. When his companions saw that he was black they swallowed hard, and then they drove with him to Tennessee.

In the South, Landsmark and his traveling companions experienced racial hatred as they never had before. At one point, Klan members chased them and they hid behind a bush. In late March 1965, Landsmark was among the thousands who marched from Selma to Montgomery. He would return south in 1968. When news of Martin Luther King's assassination hit, Landsmark instinctively got into a car and drove nonstop to attend King's funeral.

At Yale, Landsmark's thinking about social responsibility and moral accountability developed under the guidance of William Sloane Coffin, the university chaplain. A leading liberal clergyman, Coffin opposed the Vietnam War, supported civil rights, and urged peaceful acts of civil disobedience. Coffin had weekly conversations at his house about how to be an ethical and responsible individual. The group would discuss works on justice and violence and consider how best to transform an unjust society. Calvin Hill, the star football player on Yale's team who went on to a career in the NFL, was so taken by the conversations that he asked whether he should stop playing football because of the sport's violent nature. "No, no," Landsmark and the others implored.

As an undergraduate, Landsmark contemplated a career in architecture or city planning or law. As a child in the projects, he grasped intuitively the reciprocal relationship between environment and identity, but he had deep reservations about the architectural profession, which had so few black members. He did not want to spend his career in loneliness and isolation. Landsmark instead enrolled at Yale Law School and simultaneously took architecture courses. An incident with a successful Boston architect confirmed his decision. Landsmark was friends with the architect's daughter, who was getting married and invited him to the wedding. The reception was being held at a whites-only country club. The Boston architect was unhappy with the invitation of Landsmark, who attended only after the bride threatened to cancel the reception. Landsmark was left wondering whether architects had the courage to challenge discrimination.   •

In 1973, after graduating from law school, Landsmark moved to Boston and took a position at Hill & Barlow, one of the city's most prestigious firms. Michael Dukakis was his boss, and William Weld had the office across from him. Both men would one day serve as governors of the commonwealth. Ironically, the firm represented many architects, including the country club member whom Landsmark had discomfited. Landsmark quickly discovered that the mundane aspects of a law practice were not for him. Civil rights cases were one thing. But defending corporate clients such as Amtrak in railroad-crossing cases paid the bills, and after a dozen or so cases in which he negotiated a settlement with the family of some poor soul who thought he could race a train and win, Landsmark thought about moving on.

The decision to do so came easily after his first real vacation following his move to Boston in 1974. He had decided to go to the island of St. Kitts, the ancestral home of his maternal grandmother. What he found astonished him. People of African descent ran the country and were doing a terrific job. The experience was nothing less than an epiphany. The unspoken message that he had heard his whole life, that people of color could not govern without anarchy erupting, was simply not true. He realized at that moment that for all his education, and all the elite black leaders in America with whom he had had contact, he had been a victim of the pernicious effects of a racism that "inculcates and perpetuates a stereotype within the minds and culture of the people who are being discriminated against so that we come to believe that we are inferior." He returned to Boston determined to direct his life in ways that would help minorities to succeed, to manage their lives and communities from a position of confidence and strength.

Landsmark enjoyed his new position with the Contractors Association. His legal training came into play, as did his interest in civil rights and his continuing passion for architecture and environmental design. It was his work for the association that had him rushing to a meeting at City Hall on the morning of April 5, 1976.

The marchers spotted Landsmark coming toward them. So did a photographer who only minutes before had arrived on the scene.

Stanley Forman loved his job. He had shown up early for work that day, as he did every day. No news was being made in his bachelor apartment in Brighton. So Forman drove to the *Herald American* offices with his constant companion, Glossy, a golden retriever. He arrived sometime after eight for a nine-to-five shift and asked Al Salie, the assistant city editor, if anything was going on. Salie told him that Gene Dixon, another of the news photographers, was off at an anti-busing rally at City Hall. There was nothing else to do, so Forman asked if he could go join him.

He drove his silver Mercury to City Hall Plaza, about ten minutes away. He parked on the island on Cambridge Street, cracked the window for Glossy, and walked toward the plaza. It was pleasant enough for April 5; Forman took his time.

Thirty years old, Forman was a local talent who had already established himself as one of the most gifted spot news photographers in the business. He came from a working-class Jewish family in Revere, Massachusetts. His father was a musician who did not have a steady income; he played the accordion and sang at weddings and bar mitzvahs. Forman describes his mother as quiet and reserved.

Stanley Forman and Glossy
(COURTESY STANLEY
FORMAN)

He has rich memories of his childhood growing up in a two-family house in a Jewish ghetto that was known informally as the kosher canyon. He spent a fair amount of time lurking in poolrooms and drinking beer and chasing girls. One day, playing sandlot football, he dislocated his shoulder. The injury would keep him out of Vietnam.

Forman graduated from high school in 1963 but never considered college; few of his peers did. His father had bought him a camera, and Forman enjoyed fooling around with it, but he knew nothing about photography. Sometimes he would chase police and fire calls, and he even sold an occasional photo to a paper, but he had no direction.

Maybe his father knew before he did. From the time he was twelve, Forman would look over his father's shoulder at the pictures in the *Boston American*. One credit line in particular stood out for him: Rollie Oxton. Those photographs captured the boy's imagination. Urban life was an adventure, and photographers such as Oxton, who won the annual award from the Boston Press Photographers Association for best spot news photography five times, were explorers who captured on film accidents and fires and rescues.

With his father's urging, he looked up photography schools and saw an ad for the Franklin Institute of Photography. Forman enrolled in 1965. His instructor was a neighbor and local photographer who did portraits and weddings. He spent a year learning his craft: f-stops, shutter speeds, depth of field, and the mysteries of the darkroom.

In 1966, a staffer for Massachusetts attorney general Edward Brooke came to Franklin looking for a photographer to take pictures of Brooke's Senate campaign. Forman's job was to snap pictures of the candidate shaking hands with everyone he met. His first day on the job, he took scores of photographs. He stayed up late that night printing all the images in the darkroom he kept in his house. When he delivered the pictures the next day, Brooke's staff knew they had hired the right person for the job.

When Brooke was elected senator, the first African American elected since Reconstruction, Forman had doors opened to him. He wanted to remain in Boston, and he had interviews at the three dailies: the *Globe*, the *Herald*, and the *Record American*. Only Myer Ostroff, the photography editor at the *Record American*, offered Forman a chance not only to do the grunt work—clean the darkroom and file the negatives—but also to train as a spot news photographer. He went to work November 22, 1966.

A month later, he showed that he had the instincts and the work ethic to be a first-rate news photographer. A lifelong Bruins fan, Forman returned home from a game and was in bed listening to the police scanner, as he always did. He heard that a train filled with fans leaving the Boston Garden had crashed into a tanker truck. There were fatalities.

He and his father rushed to the scene. He was the first photographer there. Forman had only one roll of film. Later that night he printed the pictures. When he held up the negatives he knew he had front page material. The adrenaline rush of the chase and the excitement of beating out the competition kept him afloat for days. Some of the old-timers at the paper may have resented the kid chasing pictures when he wasn't technically working, but to everyone else he was a hero. Forman had become an action photographer. He had earned his stripes.

Forman continued to chase and continued to contribute to the pages of the *Record American*, which became the *Herald American* in 1973. He worked constantly. Before he married he would go out on a Friday night, drop off his date, then cruise while listening to the scanners that he still keeps on perpetually in his car and home. His relentless pursuit of the good news picture would contribute to the breakup of his first marriage; his wife tired of falling asleep each night to the sound of police and fire calls.

But even the hardest worker and most relentless chaser tires, and by 1975 Forman felt bored. He seemed to be in a slump; few of his pictures were making it into features, let alone onto the coveted front page. On his thirtieth birthday he went so far as to take the exam for the fire department. Less than two weeks later, on July 22, as he passed by the assignment desk, he heard a call over the fire radio for an engine to respond to a blaze. Within thirty seconds, a second alarm was sounded. People were trapped inside a burning building.

Forman raced out of the newsroom. All he knew was that the box the call came from was in the 1500 area, which meant Back Bay or South End. He picked up an engine racing to the scene and followed it. The fire was on Marlborough Street, and Forman ran to the back of the building; a district chief had been calling for a ladder truck to get there. As he arrived he saw a fireman climbing down from the roof onto the fifth-floor fire escape. A nineteen-year-old girl and her two-year-old goddaughter stood trapped by the flames inside the building.

A fire truck rolled down the alley, its ladder extended. Forman climbed onto the bed of the truck, which gave him some elevation and a better angle; in the chaos of the moment no one was bothering with a single photographer. He focused his 135-mm lens on the trio above. His camera's motor drive was on, and he began snapping pictures of what he thought would be a routine ladder rescue.

The firefighter, Robert O'Neill, shielded the other two from the flames and waited on the fire escape as the motorized ladder inched toward them. And then, just as the ladder came within reach, the fire escape collapsed. The iron came apart like a child's Erector set. O'Neill managed to grab the ladder with his left arm and pull himself to safety, but the woman and child plunged to the ground. Forman kept shooting as they fell. He took one last shot and looked away as the bodies hit with a thud.

Forman was shaking. In his years of witnessing fires and accidents and crime scenes, he had become somewhat inured to scenes of violence or death. This was different. The ambulance sped the child away; medics worked to revive the woman. As Forman left the alley he passed O'Neill, who had almost plucked them to safety. He heard the firefighter say, "Two more seconds I would have had them, two more seconds."

Forman raced back to the office. On the way he rechecked his camera to see if the exposure was as he set it: 1/250 f.8. He found his boss, Myer Ostroff, and declared, "If these pictures don't come out, I won't be in to work tomorrow and I might never come back."

Forman developed the pictures, and among them was an astonishing image of the woman and child in free fall. The composition is chilling. The woman and girl look almost as if they have voluntarily jumped. But then we realize that the fire escape has fallen off to the side, and that they and the potted plants are plunging. The victims are perfectly centered, in the photograph and in relation to one another. We see the young woman's bent left leg and it leads our eye to the girl, whose own outstretched leg shows us why they are falling. The image is sharply focused, an amazing feat given the subjects' movement.

Compelling photographs have texture, and Forman's fire escape picture is filled with shapes and angles and reflections that work together. The verticality of the picture is broken by the horizontal of the window frames and bricks and jumbled metal. Somehow, Forman's photograph creates depth, and we feel the distance of the bodies from the building and what had promised to be a means of escape.

Forman heard that night that the woman had died but the child was going to be all right. He still was not certain whether his

Stanley Forman, Fire Escape Collapse, *1975* (COURTESY STANLEY FORMAN)

pictures were any good and actually asked a friend whether or not the paper was going to run them. He did not have to wait long for his answer. He went out to another fire at two in the morning, stopped in a store, and saw the morning paper: he had the full front page and all of page three.

Fire Escape Collapse circulated around the world, appearing in well over a hundred newspapers. It generated debate and also action. Some saw it as an example of sensationalism and felt it violated journalistic ethics to print such a picture. Forman received hate mail, calling him a pervert and an opportunist. The criticism did not bother him. Many times on the scene of an accident, once he had his pictures, he had lent a helping hand. But at this one there had been nothing for him to do except his job, which was to photograph an event. Whatever the merits of showing a woman tumbling to her death—and that is an editor's, not a photographer's, decision—the photo led directly to the passage of new fire escape safety legislation in Massachusetts and across the United States.

The publisher decided to submit the series for Pulitzer Prize consideration. But executive editor Sam Bornstein warned Forman that since the *Herald American* was a Hearst paper, and Pulitzer and Hearst were rivals, it was unlikely that he would have a chance. Forman laughed. He never thought about big-shot awards such as the Pulitzer. To him, a local boy, what would have meant something was winning an award from the Boston Press Photographers Association.

In fall 1975, Forman drove with a friend to Columbia's School of Journalism in New York City to submit his pictures to the Pulitzer committee. He had dozens of clips from other papers and 16" x 20" matted pictures. The total package weighed fifteen pounds. The administrator of the Pulitzer committee met briefly with Forman and told him how wonderful the previous winner's presentation had been: a board with a single picture on it. Forman forgot about the Pulitzer and drove back to Boston.

ON THE MORNING of April 5, 1976, Forman was in no rush to arrive at yet another anti-busing rally. So he stopped to get an apple for his girlfriend, who worked around the corner from City Hall. He dropped by to chat and told her he was headed to a demonstration and would see her later.

Around ten o'clock, Forman made his way to the stairs at City Hall Plaza, exchanging greetings with various people he knew. As he looked up, he saw a large group coming down the stairs. It was no big deal. These demonstrations had become a routine occurrence. One of the protesters was waving an American flag.

Forman readied to take some shots. The protesters were moving toward him. He had two cameras, both Nikons. One had a motor drive; the other did not. He had three lenses: a 35 mm, a 135 mm, and a 20 mm in his pocket. He left the 35 on the camera without the motor drive and replaced the 135 on the other camera with the 20, which is a wide-angle lens that provides greater depth of field and therefore requires less focusing in the midst of action.

A scuffle began. The protesters spotted Landsmark and turned on him. One went to trip him up. A couple of them yelled, "Get the nigger." A few of the anti-busing protesters at the front jumped him. He was being kicked and punched. Another unidentified black man hurried away from the scene.

Joseph Rakes, the young man carrying the flag, was a few steps away from the scuffle. He circled around and began to swing the flag at Landsmark. Age seventeen, Rakes had loved school but had stopped going entirely a year into the protests against busing. He worked part-time to help his parents pay the bills, which now included tuition to send his older siblings to a private academy formed to educate those students who refused to attend South Boston or Charlestown High School. Rakes's anger at a situation beyond his control was never far from the surface. He attended most rallies against busing, and on this day he rushed into the fracas. Some officers of the police mobile operations patrol and other adults intervened, but too late. The incident lasted maybe fifteen or twenty seconds. Landsmark's glasses were shattered and his nose broken. He was left drifting, bloodied and dazed.

As Forman shot the scene, he felt the motor drive freeze; it was skipping. So he overrode it by starting to shoot single frames. He managed about twenty-three clicks. Just as suddenly as the scuffle had erupted, it ended. He didn't know what he had. In fact, he didn't think he had much. Assaults like this happened all the time and seldom made for dramatic pictures. What he knew was that most of the other photographers were caught behind the pack. Because he arrived late, Forman was in front and, of all the photographers on the scene, closest to the action. If he had been there earlier, he would have missed it.

Landsmark stumbled to his feet, and even tried to continue on to his meeting. A reporter approached him, and then veered off to cover the crowd. The police stepped in. Clarence Jones, the deputy mayor, who witnessed the assault from his office window, raced downstairs. He accompanied Landsmark to the hospital. Doctors treated the victim for contusions and a broken nose, placed a huge bandage over his face, and released him.

Other witnesses included Mayor Kevin White, who viewed the scene from his fifth-floor office: "This man, as I could see with my own eyes, had been walking calmly, quietly, and alone across City Hall Plaza right under my window when he was attacked. He was taking no part in any demonstration, yet he became a victim because he was a black man who came in contact with a bunch of hooligans."

Some of the students who did not participate—indeed, who recoiled with shock at the assault—trembled with disbelief. At the time, someone said Landsmark must have provoked the attack by making a gesture, but an incredulous Landsmark told reporters, "I didn't have time to make an obscene gesture." Several years later, Lisa McGoff, whose family was profiled by J. Anthony Lukas in his Pulitzer Prize–winning book *Common Ground*, an examination of the busing crisis told through the lives of three families, informed Lukas that she imagined that Landsmark instigated the incident. According to Lukas, McGoff's first thought as she witnessed the assault was that "this has to be a trick, because no black guy in his right mind would walk smack into the middle of an anti-busing demonstration."

But it was no trick. Landsmark told a writer who wondered how this could happen to such a well-educated and well-respected person that "I couldn't put my Yale degree in front of me to protect myself. The thing that is most troubling is that it happened not because I was somebody but because I was anybody . . . I was just a nigger they were trying to kill." To another reporter Landsmark said, "I was just out there walking to City Hall in my three-piece suit. I was anyone." And suddenly, someone tried "to kill me with the American flag."

CHAPTER 2

BOSTON AND BUSING

THE BATTLE OVER busing did not begin in Boston. Years before violence erupted in 1974, other American cities struggled with busing: Pontiac, Providence, Trenton, Detroit, Denver, Pasadena. And, of course, before the crisis turned north, southern cities wrestled over busing as a means of desegregating public schools. The battle over busing did not begin in Boston, but it was in Boston that the issue exploded in such a way that the city came to be seen as the Little Rock of the North; some even compared it to Belfast. Those sobriquets did what all nicknames do: they simplified and stereotyped. Boston's battle over busing took the shape that it did as a result of numerous competing and conflicting factors, and in the context of its own unique history.

In searching for the beginning of a story it is tempting to go back, far back, so far back that there is the danger of suffering from the disease that historian Garrett Mattingly diagnosed in his friend Bernard DeVoto: *regressus historicus*. It seems that DeVoto, the author of bestselling works on American history published in the 1940s and '50s, could not write about nineteenth-century America without going back to the sixteenth century and crossing the Atlantic to England. While we can tell the busing story without leaving this continent, there is perhaps some justification in starting as far back as

June 24, 1700, when a pamphlet condemning slavery and the slave trade was published in North America—printed in Boston.

Samuel Sewall's *The Selling of Joseph* appeared at a moment when the Massachusetts slave population had recently doubled to more than five hundred slaves, most of them in Boston. Sewall, a jurist who had come to regret his role in the Salem witch trials in 1692, was compelled to reflect on the nature of slavery when he received a petition asking him to free "a Negro and his wife, who were unjustly held in Bondage." In *The Selling of Joseph*, Sewall argued that "all men, as they are the Sons of Adam, are Coheirs; and have equal right unto liberty, and all other outward comforts of life." Sewall could not possibly imagine free blacks living in equality and side by side with whites ("they . . . remain in our body politick as a kind of extravasat blood"), and his pamphlet had no discernible impact. But that a Boston man spoke to the problems of slavery and freedom foreshadowed how essential these issues would become in the city soon to be known as the Cradle of Liberty.

The relationship between the principles of the American Revolution and the problem of slavery has long vexed scholars. "All men are created equal" seems perfectly unambiguous, and yet the phrase certainly did not lead to any mass abolitionist movement. Indeed, for many there seemed to be almost an inverse relationship between the call for liberty and the reliance on slavery. The famed British writer Samuel Johnson seized on this anomaly and inquired, "How is it that we hear the loudest yelps for liberty among the drivers of Negroes?"

In Massachusetts, as well as other northern states, the rhetoric of liberty fueled nascent anti-slavery sentiment among some politicians, and certainly among the enslaved. The Massachusetts Constitution of 1780, written by John Adams, includes a Declaration of

Rights that says, "All men are born free and equal, and have certain natural, essential, and unalienable rights; among which may be reckoned the right of enjoying and defending their lives and liberties; that of acquiring, possessing, and protecting property; in fine, that of seeking and obtaining their safety and happiness." Three years earlier, the Massachusetts General Court had received a petition from "A Great Number of Blackes detained in a State of slavery in the bowels of a free & Christian County," who set out to show "that they have in Common with all other men a Natural and Unalienable Right to that freedom which the Grat [sic] Parent of the Universe Bestowed equally on all menkind and which they have Never forfeited by any Compact or agreement whatever." By 1783, the Supreme Judicial Court had ruled in several cases that slavery was incompatible with the principles of the state constitution.

With the abolition of slavery in Massachusetts, a small but vibrant free black community began to emerge. In the early 1800s, about 1,500 blacks lived in the Beacon Hill area and parts of the West End and North End. The opening of the African Baptist Church and African Meeting House in 1806 established vital institutional structures for the growing black community that reached 2,200 (out of a population of 178,000) on the eve of the Civil War.

In antebellum America, Boston became a center of abolitionist fervor and the struggle for social reform. It was from Boston that David Walker, a free black printer and abolitionist, issued his *Appeal to the Coloured Citizens of the World* and William Lloyd Garrison, a writer, editor, and cofounder of the American Anti-Slavery Society, published the *Liberator*, a newspaper devoted to a doctrine that called for the immediate abolition of slavery. These activists were a decided minority, and their actions inflamed Boston's merchants, who profited from trade with southern slaveholders, and outraged the rising number of Irish immigrants, who objected to being dominated by Protestant moralists. Garrison faced down mobs that dragged him through the streets with a noose around his neck.

Among the issues raised by black reformers was education. William Cooper Nell, who attended Boston's Abiel Smith School, the first public school in the nation for black children, and became an apprentice printer for Garrison at the *Liberator*, petitioned the Massachusetts legislature in 1840 for school desegregation and equal rights, and he continued over the next decade to press for integration, "to hasten the day when the color of the skin would be no barrier to equal school rights." The effort made some inroads with two members of the Boston School Committee, who published a minority report in favor of integration, but schools remained segregated.

In 1849, Benjamin Roberts, a black printer, challenged the law. His daughter, Sarah, had been denied admittance to four white schools—in violation, Roberts thought, of a statute that declared children could not be unlawfully excluded from the schools. The lawyers for Roberts were Charles Sumner, who would be elected to the Senate in 1851, and Robert Morris, the leading black attorney in the city, though he was only twenty-five. Before the Supreme Court of Massachusetts, Sumner argued that no "exclusion or discrimination founded on race or color can be consistent with Equal Rights . . . There is but one Public School in Massachusetts. This is the Common School equally free to all the inhabitants. There is nothing establishing an exclusive or separate school for any particular class, rich or poor, Catholic or Protestant, white or black." In an argument one hundred years ahead of its time, Sumner insisted that there could be no such thing as equal but separate schools because "the matters taught in the two schools may be precisely the same; but a school exclusively devoted to one class, must differ essentially in spirit and character from that Common School known to the law, where all classes meet together in Equality. It is a mockery to call it an equivalent."

Chief Justice Lemuel Shaw rejected Sumner's argument: "The law has vested the power in the committee to regulate the system of distribution and classification; and when this power is reasonably exercised, without being abused or perverted by colorable pretences, the decision of the committee must be deemed conclusive. The committee, apparently upon great deliberation, have come to the conclusion, that the good of both classes of schools will be best promoted, by maintaining the separate primary schools for colored and for white children, and we can perceive no ground to doubt, that this is the honest result of their experience and judgment." Prejudice, Shaw opined, is not created by the law, and it cannot be eradicated by it.

Shaw's ruling in *Roberts v. City of Boston* would one day be taken as precedent for the "separate but equal" doctrine, but in Boston it would quickly be cast aside, as activists continued to challenge segregated schools. In 1855, with the support of the Committee on Public Instruction, the legislature passed, and the governor signed, a law that prohibited school segregation on grounds of race. A tradition of civil rights activism had been established.

In the aftermath of the Civil War, Boston continued to grow. The population reached 250,000 by 1870. A terrible fire in 1872 destroyed some eight hundred buildings on sixty-five acres of land, but the city rebuilt itself. Roxbury had been annexed in 1868, and West Roxbury, Brighton, and Charlestown in 1874. With changes in the city came shifts in neighborhoods. The small black population began to move away from Beacon Hill and by the early twentieth century congregated in Roxbury, joining Jewish and Irish residents. Only in the 1950s, fueled by the migration north of southern blacks, did Roxbury become predominantly African American. Boston's black population grew to 20,000 by 1930, 40,000 by 1950, and 63,000 by 1960, when African Americans reached a critical mass and constituted about 10 percent of the population. In 1970, there were more than 100,000 blacks out of a population of 640,000.

While Boston's black population grew slowly over time, Irish immigrants poured into Boston in the 1840s and almost immediately constituted a third of Boston's inhabitants. Settling in the North End and East Boston, these immigrants faced the prejudice of Boston's Protestant elite, who feared the changes that engulfed them. By the end of the century, the Irish rose to respectability and seized political power. They also moved out of the waterfront slums into new areas, particularly Dorchester and Charlestown and South Boston, which had been annexed in 1804. South Boston became more than a residence; it became a neighborhood that provided a powerful sense of identity to a largely white, Irish, working-class, and Catholic population of about sixty thousand by the 1950s, proud of its heritage and bonds of intimacy. That sense of separation was reinforced geographically by the Fort Point Channel, which cuts South Boston off from the rest of the city.

In the late nineteenth and early twentieth centuries, at the time of growing residential segregation, racial segregation in public facilities spread throughout the North. In 1896, *Plessy v. Ferguson*, the landmark Supreme Court case that upheld a Louisiana statute that provided for segregated public transportation, did not invent the doctrine of separate but equal; it ratified the reality of rising racism and social anxiety over the growing northern black population. In

Pennsylvania, New Jersey, New York, Illinois, Michigan, and Ohio, schools and facilities became more segregated. With the great migration of blacks out of the South following World War I, these cities became even more polarized racially, and school systems adopted even more exclusive practices.

The irony of Boston's racial history is that relatively few blacks migrated to the city from the South, and, as a result, patterns of segregation did not become more rigid, and schools remained racially mixed. Boston's seemingly benign situation in a comparatively progressive racial atmosphere had the effect of lessening the urgency of civil rights activism. Boston's NAACP, which was integrated, collapsed by 1930, a victim of tensions with the national NAACP office, internal squabbles, and conflict with William Monroe Trotter's National Equal Rights League, which spurned the paternalism of white civil rights leaders such as Oswald Garrison Villard, grandson of William Lloyd Garrison.

In the first decades of the twentieth century, Boston's racial problems—in particular, employment discrimination that prevented blacks from getting jobs on the docks or in the trade shops, and kept them in menial positions as servants or porters—no doubt contributed to keeping down the number of blacks who migrated to the city from the South. Paradoxically, the small growth in the black population kept intact a generally liberal atmosphere about race and hampered the local agenda of civil rights activists. All of that began to change after 1940 as the black population swelled and came to constitute a meaningful percentage of the city's total by 1960.

Symbolic of Boston's racial polarization after World War II was an event that took place on April 16, 1945, at Fenway Park, home of the Boston Red Sox. That day, the Red Sox held a tryout for three black baseball players: Sam Jethroe, Marvin Williams, and Jackie Robinson. By an agreement among owners, no blacks had played on a major league team since the 1880s. But World War II had helped expose racial hypocrisy in the United States and led some to call for change. Boston city councilman Isadore Muchnick compelled the Red Sox to hold the tryout by threatening not to support the waiver needed to allow teams to play on Sundays. Still, the players got the runaround and waited in Boston for days to get on the field. Wendell Smith, a black sportswriter for the *Pittsburgh Courier*, wrote, "I have three of Crispus Attucks' descendants with me," a reference to the black seaman who was killed by British soldiers at the Boston Massacre: "They are Jackie Robinson, Sammy Jethroe and Marvin Williams. All three are baseball players, and they want to play in the major leagues . . . We came here to Boston—the cradle of democracy— to see if perchance a spark of the Spirit of '76' still flickers in the hearts and minds of the owners of the Boston Red Sox and Boston Braves . . . We have been here nearly a week now, but all our appeals for fair consideration and opportunity have been in vain . . . But we are not giving up! We are Americans, the color of our skin to the contrary . . . and we are going to stick to our guns!"

The tryout lasted ninety minutes. The players left the field and never again heard from the Red Sox. As they walked off, someone from Red Sox management shouted, "Get those niggers off the field," words that echoed in Boston for decades. The Red Sox would become the last team in major league baseball to include a black player—in 1959, twelve years after Jackie Robinson broke the color line with the Brooklyn Dodgers in 1947. By then, a movement against segregation in all aspects of American life was well under way.

Northerners followed the southern resistance to desegregation with horror. The Supreme Court's 1954 decision in *Brown v. Board of Education* that "separate but equal" is inherently unequal promised to erase decades of legalized segregation and launch nothing less than a civil rights revolution. The justices relied on the findings of psychologists and sociologists showing separate educational facilities to be detrimental to the development of black children. The Court did not impose a timetable except to say, the following year, that changes should proceed with "all deliberate speed." In most communities, that meant no speed at all. The test of school desegregation came in 1957 at Central High School in Little Rock, Arkansas. The nation watched as howling, hooting crowds mobbed the nine black children chosen to attend Central High, as the governor of Arkansas defied the Supreme Court, and as the National Guard had to be called in to take the children to school and try to protect them during the day.

In the 1940s and '50s, many northern states had taken action to end explicit policies of school segregation. But only myopic northern liberals saw the problem of segregation as a southern problem. (There were plenty: on the day of the *Brown* decision one northern senator proclaimed that "the so-called 'race problem' is no problem at all for us.") In fact, northern racial separation increased between 1945 and 1965. In Pittsburgh, for example, the percentage of black children enrolled in predominantly black secondary schools rose from 23 percent to 58 percent. Even more dramatic increases were registered in Chicago, Detroit, and Philadelphia. The main reason was increasing residential segregation. The combination of massive suburban migration after World War II and a system of policies and practices that sustained and reinforced racial separation and isolation (for example, racially restrictive covenants enforced by real estate agents and racial gerrymandering of districts) created de facto segregation in the North that was as insidious as anything known in the South. Maybe even more so. By 1970, 39 percent of southern black children attended majority white schools; the figure in the North was 28 percent.

The school desegregation crisis outside of the South had certain factors in common whatever city became inflamed: patterns of residential segregation and racial practices that contributed to de facto segregation, the shifting demographics of cities, and a crisis of cultural values that had more to do with issues of social class than with race. At the same time, each city had its own local circumstances that fanned the crisis. In Boston, the political mattered as much as the social, cultural, and economic. Charter reform in 1949 had replaced a ward-based city council with an at-large city council. The attempt to destroy the old district politics of the city may have been admirable, but the effect disconnected councilors and their neighborhoods at the very moment that the black population in the city was rapidly rising. As a result, blacks had little influence on city government.

Nor did they have a presence on the Boston School Committee, a group of elected officials that dated back to the 1640s and that governed educational policy and school assignment. The committee had shown little interest in the problem of racial imbalance; indeed, its policies seemed intent on perpetuating and deepening de facto segregation. For example, in 1961, it adopted "open enrollment." Theoretically, the program would allow students to enroll in schools outside of their neighborhoods if space was available. The effect of the policy, however, was to accelerate the movement of white students out of schools with blacks, and not the integration of primarily white schools.

That same year, a revitalized and reenergized Boston chapter of the NAACP, whose Education Committee would be led by Ruth

Batson, a researcher at Boston University, asked the Massachusetts Commission Against Discrimination to investigate the issue of racial preferences and school assignments. The commission ruled that race was a not a central factor in the actions of the committee, but experience among black parents seemed to belie the conclusion.

In 1961, as the NAACP considered its next steps, a new member was elected to the School Committee. Louise Day Hicks was, in some respects, an unlikely candidate for elected office. She attended law school while in her thirties, already married and the mother of two. Projecting a genteel image, she campaigned for the School Committee promising to take the politics out and put a touch of domesticity in. "The only mother on the ballot," her slogan ran.

For two years she succeeded so well that she was elected chairwoman in January 1963. But then the system became unstable. The breakdown came after a series of meetings held between the NAACP and the Boston School Committee. Led by Ruth Batson, the NAACP sought acknowledgment from the committee that de facto segregation existed in Boston (thirteen schools were at least 90 percent black, and the budgets for those schools provided $125 less per pupil). In her statement Batson declared, "In discussion of segregation in fact in our public schools, we do not accept residential segregation as an excuse for countenancing this situation. We feel that it is the responsibility of school officials to take an affirmative and positive stand on the side of the best possible education for all children. This 'best possible education' is not possible where segregation exists."

The battle between the parties, as J. Anthony Lukas suggests in *Common Ground*, was at first semantic. The NAACP wanted acknowledgment of de facto segregation. The Boston School Committee did not pretend that all was well with the schools but would not concede the point. "It's like a picture on the wall," one member said. "Once you admit it's tipped you have to put it straight. We're not admitting anything." But what so many needed to hear was an admission of injustice, if not responsibility. On the evening of June 11, 1963, as the NAACP and the Boston School Committee met, President John F. Kennedy addressed the nation in response to Alabama governor George Wallace's blocking of the entrance to the University of Alabama: "If an American, because his skin is dark, cannot eat lunch in a restaurant open to the public, if he cannot send his children to the best public school available, if he cannot vote for public officials who represent him, if, in short, he cannot enjoy the full and free life all of us want, then who among us would be content to have the color of his skin changed and stand in his place?"

Those words resonated deep in Kennedy's hometown, among the liberals and the blacks and even members of the Boston School Committee. Louise Day Hicks had kept meeting with the NAACP, sometimes privately, to work out mutual language, and it seemed that they had agreed on a statement saying that "because of social conditions beyond our control, sections of our city have become predominantly Negro areas. These ghettos have caused large numbers of Negro children to be in fact separated from other racial and ethnic groups . . . In this city, so proud of its 'Cradle of Liberty' spirit and the home city of the President of the United States, it is only fitting and proper that we take the lead in recognizing the social revolution taking place across this nation for Negro equality."

"Fitting and proper." The phrase echoed Lincoln's Gettysburg Address: "It is altogether fitting and proper that we should do this." The southern civil rights movement had come north, and Boston had reconnected itself to its history in the struggle for freedom. But then Hicks balked. Angered at a leaked version that eliminated the phrase "beyond our control," she withdrew the statement. The NAACP was planning a one-day boycott of the schools on June 18. Hicks, angry and strident, said, "If some black leaders would rather 'play with words,' then I am indeed disillusioned."

It is naive to believe that had the original statement been released, the agony of the following decade might have been avoided. At the same time, so much of the controversy revolved around playing with words and rhetorical gamesmanship that the breakdown in discourse between parties was a political breakdown of seismic magnitude. More than eight thousand black students were absent from school on the "Stay Out for Freedom" boycott June 18. Some attended "freedom schools" set up in churches and community centers and learned about black history and the civil rights movement. Hicks, now unyielding in her position, brought new rhetoric to the crisis, words that set a tone for the pious and violent conflict of cultures that would follow: "God forgive them, for they know not what they do."

In February 1964, Boston's black children, along with students in New York, Chicago, and other northern cities, again boycotted the schools. That summer, Congress passed the Civil Rights Act, which banned discrimination, protected voters' rights, and supported actions taken to desegregate public facilities. In Massachusetts, two reports on school segregation were in the works. The first appeared in January 1965. Titled *Report on Racial Imbalance in the Boston Public Schools,* it was produced by the Massachusetts State Advisory Committee to the United States Commission on Civil Rights. The committee was chaired by Robert Drinan, a Jesuit priest and lawyer who was dean of Boston College's School of Law and would be elected to Congress in 1970, and included a subcommittee on education led by Paul Parks, an officer with Boston's NAACP. The report found de facto segregation in Boston's schools, faulted the Boston School Committee's neighborhood policies, and denounced racial imbalance in the schools because "it damages the self-confidence and motivation of Negro children," "reinforces the prejudices of children regardless of their color," and "results in a gap in the quality of educational facilities among schools."

Several months later, the Advisory Committee on Racial Imbalance in Education, appointed by Owen Kiernan, the state commissioner of education, issued its report. The committee found forty-five racially imbalanced schools in Boston, schools with more than 50 percent black enrollment. Half of the more than twenty thousand black students in the city attended twenty-eight schools that were 80 percent or more black. The report, titled *Because It Is Right—Educationally*, concluded that "racial imbalance is educationally harmful to all children" and, in particular, "does serious educational damage to Negro children by impairing their confidence, distorting their self-image, and lowering their motivation." Racial imbalance "represents a serious conflict with the American creed of equal opportunity." Drawing heavily on social science research, which, in the decade since *Brown*, had grown more sophisticated and more unanimous in finding segregated and neighborhood schools antithetical to good education, the report recommended that steps be taken to correct the imbalance. Among those to be considered: "the exchange of students between other school buildings." In other words, busing.

The Boston School Committee rejected the report, and Hicks seized on the one recommendation about busing and denounced it as "undemocratic, un-American, absurdly expensive and diametrically opposed to the wishes of the parents in this city." She labeled the committee members "a small band of racial agitators, non-native to Boston, and a few college radicals who have joined the conspiracy to tell the people of Boston how to run their schools, their city and their lives."

With the Kiernan report and the Boston School Committee response, what had started as semantic differences over the phrase "de facto segregation" metastasized into a deep-rooted cultural conflict in which both sides claimed to stand for an American tradition. It was a conflict in which cosmopolitanism and localism, liberalism and populism, butted against each other. Boston had a long tradition of activism and support of civil rights, and it had a long tradition of self-determination and ethnic pride. Both were in the ascendant in the 1960s; in the crisis over busing, they would be at war.

Motivated by the reports on racial imbalance, and inspired by Martin Luther King's visit to Boston on April 22–23—a visit in which King admitted it would be "dishonest to say Boston is Birmingham" but "irresponsible for me to deny the crippling poverty and the injustice that exist in some sections of this community," a visit in which King proclaimed that "Boston must become a testing ground for the ideals of freedom"—the state legislature passed the Racial Imbalance Act.

The act, the first of its kind in the nation, defined "racial imbalance" as a ratio between nonwhite and other students in public schools "which is sharply out of balance with the racial composition of the society in which non-white children study, serve and work." It deemed racial imbalance to exist when the percentage of nonwhite students exceeded 50 percent of the total number of students in a school. If the School Committee failed to take action to eliminate the imbalance, the schools would lose millions of dollars in state aid to education.

The legislature's desire to do something about de facto segregation may have been admirable, but the statewide act was passed with only one Boston representative voting for it. Hicks and other members of the Boston School Committee would make much of local communities being dictated to by legislators from outside of Boston who could easily vote their conscience when the results of their vote would have no impact on their suburban constituencies. "I am tired," Hicks declared, "of nonresidents telling the people of Boston what they should do." For years, the committee challenged the act legally and found ways to undercut its intent through policies of student assignment, enrollment management, and school construction. Over time, the state board of education withheld more than fifty million dollars in funds, and the number of schools defined as imbalanced rose from forty-five in 1965 to sixty-two in 1971.

Dismayed by the recalcitrance of the School Committee, which in August 1965 reversed an agreement to bus some students from overcrowded schools in Roxbury and North Dorchester to Brighton and Dorchester, black parents helped organize their own programs. The North Dorchester–Roxbury Parent Association, for example, took advantage of the open enrollment policy to bus black children to open seats in white schools. Called Operation Exodus and funded by the NAACP, labor unions, and money raised by parents, the program bused more than five hundred students by 1967. Even more successful was the Metropolitan Council for Educational Opportunity (METCO), founded in 1966. Funded by grants from the federal government and the Carnegie Corporation, METCO bused inner-city black students in Boston to suburban schools. The state soon took over funding of the program, which cost two million dollars, and by 1974 was sending twenty-five hundred black children to superior schools in more than thirty suburbs.

But sending black children to the suburbs was not a way of

carrying out the desegregation of Boston's schools. The Racial Imbalance Act said that Boston's schools had to desegregate; the Boston School Committee said that the segregation that existed was caused by residential and neighborhood patterns, not systematic discrimination, and that a solution was improvement of majority-black schools, not busing. To date, the discussion had been emotional but civil. The mayoral campaign of 1967, in which Louise Day Hicks ran as a candidate, polarized the sides and blurred the lines between arguments for local self-determination and racist demagoguery.

Hicks drew national attention when, in a September primary election, she beat nine male opponents, with 28 percent of the total and 50 percent more votes than runner-up Kevin White, with whom she would face a runoff. Even the Boston Red Sox in the World Series did not steal attention away from her. Taking her overwhelming reelection to the School Committee in 1963, and again in 1965, as a mandate, she ran, she said, "as a symbol of resistance." To be sure, she was resisting desegregation ("You know where I stand" became a campaign motto), but she was also resisting being told what to do by the federal government, the state, and an assortment of activists who, she felt, did not necessarily represent the desires of the black community, much less the poor white working class who remained in a city that over the decades had seen its population plummet because of middle-class flight to the suburbs. Asked to explain Hicks's popularity, one political observer said, "Most of the people who would have voted against Mrs. Hicks 10 years ago have moved out to Wellesley, Brookline and Newton." Hicks was a one-issue candidate, and other interests in Boston united to give Kevin White, a well-connected politician, the victory. Still, Hicks had mobilized her base, a proud, patriotic group of people who had watched their economic status decline, felt deep ties to their local community, disdained the riots that had engulfed the nation (Watts, Newark, Detroit, even Roxbury), and resented all the effort on behalf of black rights. Asked about Hicks, one constituent said: "It's not so much she's anti-Negro as it is she's for the white people. And why not? There was no civil rights when our people were coming up."

By 1970, the debate did not focus on the problem of desegregation but on the problem of busing. Before busing became identified as a Boston issue, it exploded as a national trauma. On April 20, 1971, the Supreme Court issued its decision in *Swann v. Charlotte-Mecklenburg Board of Education*. Darius Swann, a theology professor, sued the school board when his six-year-old son was prevented from attending a local integrated elementary school. Despite a desegregation plan put in place in 1965, two thirds of the twenty-one thousand black students in Charlotte attended twenty-one schools that were almost exclusively black. The Court was determined, seventeen years after *Brown*, to articulate the guidelines by which school authorities would "eliminate from the public schools all vestiges of state-imposed segregation." Writing for a unanimous Court, Chief Justice Warren Burger discussed the importance of such issues as constructing new schools and closing old ones, the allocation of resources, the assignment of faculty as well as students, and transportation. On this last issue the Court observed: "Bus transportation has been an integral part of the public education system for years, and was perhaps the single most important factor in the transition from the one-room schoolhouse to the consolidated school. Eighteen million of the Nation's public school children, approximately 39%, were transported to their schools by bus in 1969–1970 in all parts of the country." The Court concluded that "we find no basis for holding that the local school authorities may not be required to employ bus transportation as one tool of school desegregation. Desegregation plans cannot be limited to the walk-in school."

The Supreme Court may have given its support to busing as a remedy for achieving desegregation, but polls suggested that more than 80 percent of the American people opposed busing. In Pontiac, Michigan, in August 1971, protesters dynamited a half dozen buses sitting at a depot. In San Francisco, Rochester, and other cities, parents organized in opposition to busing plans. The comments of the president emboldened the protesters: Richard Nixon declared, "I have consistently opposed the busing of our Nation's schoolchildren to achieve a racial balance, and I am opposed to the busing of children simply for the sake of busing." The White House proposed a constitutional amendment banning busing, and Congress regularly debated the issue while taking other actions, such as prohibiting the use of federal funds for busing, to show its disdain.

On November 15, 1971, *Time*'s cover article was titled "The Agony of Busing Moves North." The editors trod cautiously, trying to be fair to all sides: "it is doubtful that white parents have so strong a right to choose a specific public school for their children, but it is even more doubtful that they should be forced by law to have their offspring bused where their safety is endangered or where they will demonstrably suffer along educational lines." Still, busing was needed, they thought, because "until bad schools improve and neighborhoods integrate, to outlaw busing would be to run the risk that the dangerous gulf between two nations—one black, one white— could grow even wider."

In March 1972, dismayed by the lack of progress being made against the Boston School Committee in the state courts, the NAACP, on behalf of fifty-three plaintiffs, filed suit in federal court against the Boston School Committee. Tallulah Morgan was listed as the first plaintiff, and James Hennigan was chairman of the Boston School Committee. Judge W. Arthur Garrity Jr., a graduate of Holy Cross and Harvard Law and confirmed to the district court in 1966, was chosen to hear the case of *Morgan v. Hennigan*. It would have taken any judge time to work through the issues and case law, but Garrity was not any judge. He was meticulous, thorough, and exacting. J. Anthony Lukas noted that "unlike other judges, who delegated heavily to young law clerks, Garrity read everything that crossed his desk, often working twelve hours a day, and such diligence meant that years might go by before he decided a complex case."

Morgan v. Hennigan required Garrity to go back to the 1950s to review the actions of the Boston School Committee and the state board of education. It required him to familiarize himself with court actions since *Brown*, not only at the federal but also at the state level, cases from cities all over the country—including Springfield in 1964, where a district court judge ruled against de facto segregation but was reversed by the Court of Appeals. It required him to read countless filings, hear testimony over a two-week trial, and stay abreast of new developments that seemed to be emerging almost daily. For example, a year into the case, the Supreme Court decided in *Keyes v. School District No. 1, Denver, Colorado* that "unlawful segregative design on the part of school authorities," even where schools had not been segregated by law, was impermissible. Finally, the case required that, in the event he found in favor of the plaintiffs, there was a remedy for him to impose.

After more than two years, on June 21, 1974, Garrity handed down his decision, which ran more than 150 pages. Systematically and methodically he inched toward a conclusion. He noted: "Eighty-four percent of Boston's white students attend schools that are more than 80% White; 62% of the black students attend schools that are more than 70% Black. At least 80% of Boston's schools are segregated in the sense that their racial compositions are sharply out of line with the racial composition of the Boston public school system as a whole." The question was how it got that way, and the answer, Garrity ruled, touched on every aspect of the school system including enrollment patterns, districting, feeder systems, allocation of resources, and distribution of faculty. Drawing on the transcripts of Boston School Committee meetings, among other sources, Garrity found members deliberately dragging their feet, rationalizing their actions, and employing explicitly racial reasons for their decisions, all designed, he believed, to perpetuate segregation. By the time he was done, his conclusion was inescapable, as much axiom as opinion: "The defendants have knowingly carried out a systematic program of segregation affecting all of the city's students, teachers and school facilities and have intentionally brought about and maintained a dual school system. Therefore the entire school system of Boston is unconstitutionally segregated."

Because Garrity's decision came with less than three months to go before school started, there was no time for him to construct a remedy. As a result, in this first phase of the decision (Phase II would come a year later, in September 1975), he chose as the remedy a plan proposed by the state board of education and already ordered to be implemented by the Supreme Judicial Court of Massachusetts as a result of a state lawsuit that had been decided in October 1973. That plan was designed by Charles Glenn, an Episcopal priest and civil rights activist who, in 1971, had been appointed the head of a newly created Bureau of Equal Educational Opportunity. The plan called for reducing the number of imbalanced schools by half by busing some seventeen thousand students. Its most controversial element left South Boston and Roxbury paired for cross-busing. Educators at the time knew this was a toxic mixture. South Boston had been the center of opposition to busing for nearly ten years. And the students of South Boston and Roxbury were among the poorest in the city. Advisors to the state, such as Louis Jaffe of Harvard Law School, warned early in 1973 that "this part of the plan should be restudied," but it was not, and Garrity implemented it—though he admitted from the bench that he had not studied it. Perhaps he had not even read it. Having labored so hard to reach a decision, it seems Garrity's thoroughness of purpose abandoned him when it came to choosing a remedy. South Boston's William Bulger, repeatedly elected to the Massachusetts House in 1961 and, starting in 1970, the Senate, and a leading opponent of busing, later said that Garrity had "the sensitivity of a chain saw and the foresight of a mackerel."

Garrity's decision came at a moment when the opposition to busing was intensifying. On the national scene, the House of Representatives on March 26, 1974, voted for a constitutional amendment that prohibited busing. On the state scene, the Massachusetts legislature voted in October 1973 to repeal the Racial Imbalance Act, and although the governor vetoed the action, he subsequently supported an amendment of the act that substantially diluted it. On the local scene, in February 1974, Louise Day Hicks, now back on the City Council after spending one term in Congress, and State Representative Raymond Flynn, formed Massachusetts Citizens Against Forced Busing—a group that, along with the Save Boston Committee, would be absorbed into the overarching anti-busing organization

Restore Our Alienated Rights (ROAR). "Save Boston Day," a rally held on April 3 at the statehouse, drew thousands of people. Mayor White expressed the seemingly contradictory position of many Bostonians when he said, "I'm for integration, but am against forced busing."

Not only was busing anathema, but some had even begun to question the assumption that desegregation was educationally beneficial to black children and that education could serve as a vital tool for transforming society. Ever since *Brown*, which cited "a feeling of inferiority" that might afflict blacks in segregated schools, the assumption that black children profited educationally from integrated classrooms had been an article of faith. In 1966, a report issued by sociologist James Coleman, *Equality of Educational Opportunity,* tested this conviction, and, in fact, many of his findings challenged the belief. For example, Coleman discovered that issues of class and family had far more impact on educational achievement than differences in schools, which he found to be fewer than expected. But almost no one at the time seized on these results. Instead, educators and activists read and codified those parts of the report indicating that black students performed poorly compared to white students and predicting improved test scores for black children in integrated classrooms. The following year, a report issued by the United States Commission on Civil Rights, *Racial Isolation in the Public Schools*, concluded that "Negro children suffer serious harm when their education takes place in public schools which are racially segregated."

By the early 1970s, however, a "crisis of doubt" had emerged about the equalizing benefits of education and the means to attain them. David J. Armor, a Harvard sociologist, specifically studied the evidence on busing and education and found that "busing is *not* an effective policy instrument for raising the achievement of black students or for increasing interracial harmony." Integration, he argued, did not have an effect on academic achievement or aspirations for college and future occupations. The data even suggested that rather than "reduce racial stereotypes, increase tolerance, and generally improve race relations . . . integration heightens racial identity and consciousness, enhances ideologies that promote racial segregation, and reduces opportunities for actual contact between the races."

These were disturbing conclusions that raised fundamental questions about the relationship between public policy and social science. Not surprisingly, other sociologists found fault with Armor's study, arguing that he presented selected findings, his work suffered from methodological problems, and he held too high a standard for what constituted achievement. Whatever the merits of the argument, at the precise moment Garrity was preparing to issue his decision, the social assumptions that underlie *Brown* were under assault, and the opponents of busing had found unexpected support for their position.

On September 12, 1974, the first day of school, the students and parents who gathered outside South Boston High School did not need a Harvard sociologist, or the president of the United States, for that matter, to confirm for them what they had known for years: busing would not work, probably not anywhere, but certainly not in their community. They called it forced busing—forced on them against parental control and will; forced on them by academics and activists who lived outside the community; forced on them by residents of the suburbs (who themselves had recently been exempted from desegregation orders by the Supreme Court in *Milliken v. Bradley*, a Detroit case); forced on them by the media, especially the *Globe*, which became anathema to anti-busing activists; in sum,

forced on them by "unaffected proponents" for whom making a so-
ciological experiment of poor black and white working-class students
was easy, since their own children were not involved. And it wasn't
only South Boston and Charlestown that were opposed. There were
parents in Roxbury who had begun to wonder about the benefits of
integration, who had been drawn to the black power movement, and
who thought that better schools and teachers and curriculum in
their own neighborhoods would provide the education they as parents sought for their children.

On September 12, 1974, an upheaval that had been developing
for over a decade—or maybe longer, all the way back to the beginnings of Boston's long history of race relations—had arrived. It came
out of good intentions, and good intentions gone awry, and some intentions that were not so good to begin with. It came out of some
circumstances that were national in scope and some that were purely
local. It came out of demographic shifts, steadfast beliefs, and failures
of leadership on many different levels. The crisis hit in the form of a
federal court order. And yet, as meager as the preparations had been
in the three months since Garrity's decision, at seventy-nine of the
eighty schools affected by the court's decision, the buses rolled without major incident. At South Boston High School, however, the crisis
unleashed hatred and violence that threatened to destroy the city.

On that first day, 66 percent of the students in Boston attended
school, but at South Boston High School, out of an expected total
enrollment of 1,539 (797 black), there were 68 white students and 56
black students. At Roxbury, 13 white students attended. As the buses
rolled into South Boston, they were greeted by a crowd of several
hundred chanting "Here we go, Southie." Racist graffiti had been
painted on the school walls. Someone threw a rock in the morning,

and more rocks, bricks, and eggs were thrown in the afternoon. "Get those niggers out of our school," shrieked one protester. Some carried signs that read BUS 'EM BACK TO AFRICA. The Progressive Labor Party was also there, with a sign that read FIGHT RACISM, FIGHT THE BOSSES. Many protesters did not like the Progressives any more than any other outsider, and fists flew. Some photographers found themselves under assault as well. The police, many of them from the very neighborhood now under siege, had an impossible job to do and under trying circumstances tried to preserve order the best that they could. Politicians and editors, seeking to cast events in a positive light, characterized the day as "generally peaceful" and "a fine beginning." But it was clear that the protesting, chanting, and pelting had only just begun.

Newspapers across the country took note. The *Dallas Times Herald* observed that "it must be one of the greatest ironies of our time when black children quietly and peacefully board buses to desegregate schools in Selma, Atlanta, Richmond and Dallas, but are stoned in Boston." In Little Rock, the *Arkansas Gazette* said that busing was being used as an excuse by northern segregationists: "In Boston as in Little Rock an adequate desegregation of schools cannot be accomplished without transporting a portion of the pupil population to schools not in their immediate neighborhood." Closer to home, the *Hartford Courant* did not excuse the behavior but explained it in terms of class, not race: "South Boston's Irish certainly are not opposed to blacks solely because of color difference. Nor is their concern only with schools, they also fear competition with blacks over jobs, housing and social services." Whatever the volatile mixture of racial hatred and class resentment, the *Boston Globe* lamented that "Boston was supposed to be an enlightened city, the

Athens of America. Now our collective conscience is stunned by bru-tal attacks on children in school buses and on innocent citizens go-ing about their business on our streets."

After another day in which attendance dropped and boycotts and protests continued, the weekend arrived. On Monday, anti-busing leaders Louise Day Hicks, Michael Flaherty, and William Bulger issued a "Declaration of Clarification." Seeking to defend South Boston against the accusation that its residents were all racist, the authors denounced "the vicious impression that they are a people opposed to black people and their legitimate aspirations." At the same time, the declaration made it clear that they were afraid of "crime-infested Roxbury," where "there are at least one hundred black people walking around in the black community who have killed white people during the past two years." Seeking to offset the caricature of South Boston as occupied by violent Irish hooligans, the hastily prepared statement perpetuated its own caricature of Roxbury as peopled by a criminal underclass. Black parents and white dreaded sending their children into hostile territory, and the stereotypes of South Boston and Roxbury spread by journalists and politicians, and reinforced by racial assaults in both districts, deep-ened the crisis.

White and black liberals who supported busing may have felt in some way that this was their civil rights movement, some ten years after the memorable marches and protests led by Martin Luther King, but it was the anti-busing activists who employed the tactics of the civil rights movement by organizing school boycotts, holding prayer vigils, and engaging in acts of nonviolent protest that led to arrests. Jim Kelly, of the South Boston Information Center, recalled that "a lot of what we did was copped from the peaceful demonstrations of the civil rights movement." He claimed never to condone or be involved in threats or violence, but he was also unable to keep the crowds under control.

The violence, and rumors of violence, escalated and spread. There were incidents not only at South Boston High School but at Hyde Park, North Dorchester, and Roslindale. The presence of the Tactical Police Force (TPF) in South Boston further inflamed the residents, who felt under siege by officers, some of whom were themselves residents. And with Boston as the national story, groups descended on South Boston, not only progressive groups but racist ones such as the National Socialist White People's Party and David Duke's Knights of the Ku Klux Klan, groups repudiated by the residents of South Boston in no uncertain terms. Each day was another obstacle course to be navigated by parents and police, protesters and politicians, students and administrators. Attendance fluctuated based on what was taking place. On October 2, the first of many riots inside South Boston High School occurred when a shoving match in the cafeteria turned into lunch trays flying and rumors of worse. "Mass hysteria" is how one teacher described it. The following day, nearly two hundred fewer students came to school. And the next day, with major anti-busing demonstrations held, citywide school attendance dropped to 51 percent.

At times, the violence turned life-threatening. A brick found its way through a TPF windshield, and a local South Boston establishment and its patrons got payback. A Haitian man drove his car on the wrong block at the wrong time and nearly died when he was dragged from the vehicle and severely beaten. A white student at Hyde Park High School was knifed; two months later it happened again at South Boston High School, an event that nearly led to a full-blown race riot and shut down the high school for almost a month. For every action there was a reaction, and retaliation often became the only objective. The governor called for federal marshals or the National Guard, but the requests were refused. President Gerald Ford did not help ease tensions when he announced on October 10, "I have consistently opposed forced busing to achieve racial balance as a solution to quality education and, therefore, I respectfully disagree with the judge's order." Whatever the president was thinking, his words gave sustenance to those who were resisting peacefully as well as those operating outside of the law. "Open guerilla warfare" is how one official described the scene in South Boston and Roxbury.

On March 5, 1975, some four hundred anti-busing protesters attended a reenactment of the Boston Massacre. They conducted a mock funeral procession behind a coffin carrying the corpse of Liberty with a sign attached: RIP B. 1776–D. 1974." YOU THINK THIS IS A MASSACRE, JUST WAIT, read one placard. BOSTON MOURNS ITS LOST FREEDOM, read another sign. They chanted, "Garrity's killed liberty." Garrity's tyrannical court order, in their eyes, was comparable to the tyranny of Parliament and King two hundred years earlier. During the reenactment, when shots were fired, the protesters all fell to the ground. A black man had been among the original victims of the Boston Massacre in 1770, but not here, not at this reenactment.

One of the ugliest incidents occurred on April 6 when, after visiting a school in Quincy, Senator Edward Kennedy came under attack. Kennedy supported desegregation and urged his constituents to obey the law. Moreover, he was close to Garrity, who was denounced at times as "Kennedy's puppet." This was not the first time protesters turned on him. At a rally on September 9, 1974, he was shouted down and had tomatoes thrown at him. Now, at Quincy, a crowd of two to three hundred not only jeered and taunted but slashed the tires of his car and threw rocks. And at least one person turned her American flag against him. According to one editorial, "the irony of this exhibition of un-American conduct was blatantly illustrated by the action of a woman in the crowd. As she bombarded Kennedy with abusive language, she kept jabbing at him with the point of a small American flag standard."

However much protesters embraced the flag, it became increasingly difficult for opponents of busing to defend against the charge not only of being un-American but also racist. The venom of John Kerrigan, chairman of the Boston School Committee since 1968, who according to journalists referred to blacks as "savages" and once said of a black reporter that "he was one generation away from swinging in the trees," did much to cast all busing opponents as racists. Kerrigan continually called for a metropolitan solution to the problem of segregated schools, asking, "Isn't racial isolation of white students in suburbia every bit as damaging and insidious" as the racial isolation of blacks? In response, educators such as Jonathan Kozol denounced Kerrigan for using the idea of busing to the suburbs as "a mask for his racist policies."

The fear, violence, and racism reinforced one another. Some saw in the pattern a long history in America of using and manipulating race in such a way as to divide those with common class interests. "The Irish have much to learn through the association of their children with blacks," wrote one minister. "They might discover that their real enemy is the system that has kept them in the ghetto of South Boston, as it has kept blacks in the ghetto of Roxbury." The distinguished Harvard psychiatrist Robert Coles, who had studied the debilitating effects of segregation on children, offered a similar

Man with flag, c. 1976 (NORTHEASTERN UNIVERSITY ARCHIVES AND SPECIAL COLLECTIONS)

analysis: "The ultimate reality is the reality of class, having and not having, social and economic vulnerability versus social and economic power—that's where the issue is."

But the issue of class—of the inner city versus the suburbs—never had the traction some anti-busing leaders hoped for. State Senator William Bulger despaired over "the burden of public contempt and ridicule . . . growing out of the unremitting, calculated, unconscionable portrayal of each of us . . . as unreconstructed racists." Desiring "to assert the natural rights of parents to safeguard the education of their children in their traditional local schools does not mean," he declared, "that we oppose the ideals of integrated education . . . It does not mean that we are rejecting the ideals of the brotherhood of man under the fatherhood of God."

How to achieve the ideal was the rub. All through the year, Garrity was trying to plan for Phase II of the desegregation of the schools, to go into effect in September 1975. The Boston School Committee, ordered to submit a plan, refused to do so after the stabbing at South Boston High School. Other groups were not as unwilling, and Garrity received plans from the state, from the NAACP, and from a group of special masters and experts he had selected. The Masters' Plan, which divided the city into nine community school districts and would have reduced busing, eliminating it between South Boston and Roxbury, seemed promising and received a favorable response from most quarters of the city. The *Boston Globe* praised it as following in the tradition of Solomon. But on May 10, 1975, when Judge Garrity issued his order for Phase II, he had revised the Masters' Plan in such a way that rather than decreasing busing, it actually increased it from fewer than fifteen thousand students to more than twenty-two thousand.

No one was happy. The mayor expressed regret and disappointment. The NAACP thought too much of the burden of desegregation fell on the black community. The Boston School Committee called it a "disaster." Hicks accused Garrity of creating a "legal monstrosity" that would accelerate middle-class white flight to the suburbs and establish the very entity he sought to eliminate: a racially divided city. At the moment of Garrity's decision, a new report issued by James Coleman, whose original study a decade earlier was used to justify busing, concluded that "programs of desegregation have acted to further separate blacks and whites rather than bring them together" and that "busing does not work." Parents received in the mail a booklet from the court explaining their options under Phase II and were given eight days to make their decisions. They felt pressured and confused. The first school year under a court order for desegregation had come to an end. The second did not promise to go any better.

In September 1975, not only were there the usual spasms of protest and violence, but now Charlestown, which demographically was akin to South Boston and had been excluded from busing in Phase I, also entered the fray. On the first day, only 315 of the 883 students assigned to Charlestown High attended. At the end of the month, teachers throughout the city went on strike over their contract and established picket lines outside the schools. It was settled within a week, but attendance took another hit. Headmasters might declare on the morning address system, "Remember, you're here to learn. That's the purpose of this school," but few actually believed that there was any meaningful learning taking place.

In November, Judge Garrity began to hold evidentiary hearings to determine whether the court's desegregation order was being implemented at South Boston High School. After taking testimony from students and administrators, and personally visiting the high school twice, Garrity ruled on December 9 that the Boston School Committee would no longer run the school. Instead, it would be placed in receivership and run by the court. He also ordered the headmaster, Dr. William Reid, and administrative staff transferred. A national search for a new headmaster for South Boston High School led to the appointment on April 1 of Jerome Winegar from St. Paul, Minnesota, where he had established a reputation as an innovative and progressive educator.

Winegar's appointment was opposed by teachers and parents who thought that Dr. Reid had been treated unfairly and who were smarting over the high school being placed under direct control of the court. The battle over busing seemed to be turning. Garrity's decisions were being upheld by higher courts. A year earlier, Garrity had allowed three intransigent School Committee members who refused to adhere to his order to submit a desegregation plan to avoid fines for civil contempt, and his decision served only to encourage militant opposition by the majority of the committee. No more; the judge had had enough.

To protest Garrity's actions and Winegar's appointment, and to call for an end to busing, students at Charlestown High and South Boston High organized a boycott of classes on Monday, April 5. That day, one teacher at South Boston "worked individually with the black students" because there were no white students in her class. The students and chaperones traveled to City Hall Plaza, where they were greeted warmly by Louise Day Hicks and recited the Pledge of Allegiance. They filed outside into the mild morning air. At that moment, a black man came into view. Then, in one click of a photographer's shutter, the anti-busing claim that the movement was not driven by racism, and that protesters were patriotic defenders against tyranny, came undone.

CHAPTER 3

THE PHOTOGRAPH

IN THE IMMEDIATE aftermath of the incident on April 5, Forman had no idea whether he had any newsworthy images, and he was in no rush to get back to the office. As he walked around the Federal Building, down by Post Office Square, he ran into a *Herald American* reporter, Joe Driscoll. Driscoll asked, "Did you hear what happened at City Hall? A black guy got beat up by a flag."

"I got it," Forman replied.

Driscoll screamed, "What! You got it? You better get in the office."

Forman retrieved his car and returned to the office sometime before noon.

He went to the darkroom and developed the pictures. He had two choices: do it by hand, bathing the negatives in chemicals, or put the film through a Versamat machine, which quickly developed the negatives but every so often turned those negatives to confetti.

Forman was impatient to see what he had. He did not like the printing process and had little desire to make magic in the darkroom by playing with contrasts. He always just wanted to get in and get back out. "You do not have the picture until you see the developed negative" is a truth every photographer lives by. Once, early in his career, Forman took some shots, entered the darkroom, and discovered that he had forgotten to load film in the camera. He hated the darkroom, so, despite the risk of his roll being eaten, he fed it through the machine.

The pictures came out unharmed, and Forman went to the light table. He looked at them and did not get overly excited. In that moment of first seeing what he had, he did not recognize the power of one of those images.

But as the editors gathered in the afternoon, excitement and nervousness began to build. Every day at five o'clock they met to lay out the paper. An argument ensued over whether to run Forman's photograph. One editor urged against it, fearing that it would inflame racial tensions and cause riots. But Myer Ostroff, head of the photo department, and other editors, argued that it had to run on page one.

The national story that day was the death of Howard Hughes. Sam Bornstein, the executive editor, knew that the headline and the top half of the front page would be devoted to Hughes. But the local story was the anti-busing movement, and the *Herald American* was a city newspaper. Before the editors' meeting broke, Bornstein had made his decision. The disturbing, potentially explosive photo of a protester using an American flag as a weapon against a black man would make page one.

By featuring Forman's photograph, editors were doing what editors had been doing with photographs for decades: using them to help sell newspapers. Although photography first appeared with the daguerreotype in 1839, technological restraints made use of the camera to record events impractical. Lengthy exposure times and cumbersome equipment allowed only for portraits or images of still subjects: this in part explains the popularity of pictures of the dead in nineteenth-century photography. Even during the Civil War, technology did not allow photographers to capture action. There are thousands of images of the era, but nearly all are of battlefields and armaments and soldiers in fixed positions.

By the end of the century, dramatic changes had taken place. The daguerreotype, a one-of-a-kind original, gave way to film processes that produced a negative, and those processes themselves became refined with the creation in the 1870s of the dry plate process, which meant photographs did not have to be developed immediately. A decade later, plates gave way to rolls of film. At the same time, the size of the camera shrank. In the 1880s, George Eastman introduced a camera with the slogan "You press the button—we do the rest." By century's end, the "Brownie" camera ("operated by any school boy or girl") went on the market for one dollar, and photography became a national hobby and obsession. These light, portable cameras allowed snapshots to be taken of everything and everyone. For children, the camera might have been an elaborate toy. But for journalists, it became an indispensable tool.

While we remember most of the muckraking journalists of the turn of the twentieth century for their writings—Lincoln Steffens, Ida Tarbell, Upton Sinclair—others seized on the power of the camera to reveal and tell a story. In 1890, Jacob Riis published *How the Other Half Lives*, a book of words and pictures depicting life among the poor of New York. His camera, with a new accessory, flash powder, exposed the darkest places of the city. Perhaps most significant of all, a new printing technology, the halftone process, allowed for the first time the reproduction of photographs in books, magazines, and newspapers. Invented in the 1880s, the technique divided a photograph into thousands of black dots by covering it with a screen and rephotographing it. The pattern of dots could then be printed in a book or magazine.

Prior to the halftone process, only engraved images such as woodcuts appeared in print. The cultural transformation ushered in by the halftone process cannot be exaggerated: photographic reality became everyday reality, and photographs became an indispensable part of reporting the news. In 1897, the *New York Tribune* became the first newspaper to use photographs on a regular basis, and muckraking magazines such as *McClure's* also relied on photographs as evidence for the stories they reported. Photography and the news went hand in hand, as evidenced by the shots of the aftermath of the earthquake of 1906 that appeared in the *San Francisco Examiner*. Photographs themselves became news as photographers competed for exclusives, and front page pictures helped sell newspapers. On January 12, 1928, Thomas Howard, a photographer for New York's *Daily News*, which has a camera icon in its logo, sneaked a miniature camera into Sing Sing and snapped a photograph of Ruth Snyder at the moment of her electrocution. The image appeared on the front page the next day, and the paper is said to have printed an extra 750,000 copies to meet the demand. In 1936, Henry Luce began publishing *Life*, a weekly photojournalism magazine that, over nearly forty years, did as much to shape American culture as to document it.

The Pulitzer Prize Board first awarded an annual prize for photography in 1942. In 1968 they split the prize into two: spot news photography and feature photography. Forman was a spot news photographer, and it was for spot news that he submitted both *Fire Escape Collapse* and *The Soiling of Old Glory* for Pulitzer consideration.

Whereas Forman stood alone in the back of the building when he shot the fire in Back Bay, he was one of several photographers on the scene when Landsmark was attacked. Comparing his photograph as it appeared in the *Herald American* with the picture in the *Globe* underscores the visual drama that Forman alone captured that day. It also illustrates the competition between the dailies and the way editors used photographs not only to report the news but also to help sell papers.

Editors featured Forman's photograph at the center of page one. The death of Howard Hughes may have been the lead, but the composition of the front page draws the eye to the center photograph and the headline "Youths Beat Black Lawyer at City Hall." The photograph itself is cropped at the top, making the scene even more compressed and claustrophobic. The powerful diagonal thrust of the flag cuts not only the picture but the page in half. It stands above the fold. Using a second, square Forman photograph below it boxes in the central picture and adds additional force to the page. The two photographs are out of sequence: the kicking of Landsmark occurred before the assault with the flag. The arrangement may have deceived viewers, but in selling papers drama trumps chronology.

The *Globe* photographer, Ed Jenner, found himself along with the other media behind the marchers when the melee broke out. His photograph shows Landsmark being punched, but the image is not particularly dramatic. There are too many people in the center of the scene. The flag is in the background, but it plays no role in the composition. Jenner's photograph shows a moment before the attack with the flag. It was the clearest picture of the assault that he got, but the image carries little impact, if only because the viewer has to work too hard to make any sense of the scene. The *Globe*'s editors placed the story at the bottom of page one with the headline "Black Man Beaten by Young Busing Protesters." On this day, the *Herald* had beaten the *Globe*.

Examining the position of *The Soiling of Old Glory* on the front page of the *Herald American* is only one aspect of reading the image. Forman's photograph is a masterful picture not simply because of what it depicts and where it appeared but because of how it is composed. Several photographers took pictures of the incident at City Hall Plaza, but only Forman took a picture that seems historic, an image that we feel as much as we see. It is worth asking what makes Forman's photograph so powerful. How do we read *The Soiling of Old Glory*?

One place to begin is with the visual textures of the image. It seems a bit blurry. Indeed, because he was shooting at a relatively slow shutter speed of 1/250, there is subject movement in all the frames, but the effect is to enhance the sense of frenzy. The play of light and dark is essential to the scene. The steel shaft's bright line of white splits the picture in half and draws our eye to the literal center. The photograph is slightly out of focus but for the tip of the shaft, which hangs in suspended animation. The flag bearer's dark clothes place the pole and flag in relief: the whiteness of the stars and stripes in the foreground is mirrored by the pulsing brightness of the background. Because of the 20 mm lens, there is some distortion at the edges and Rakes appears a bit elongated, making him look even more menacing. The event drama of white against black is replayed in the visual drama of light against darkness: the plaid shirt and white pants of the youth in the center, the white shirt of the man turning away, Landsmark's white sleeve from his rumpled suit. The stream of light carries our eye across the scene, from left to right, just

Boston Herald American, *April 6, 1976* (COURTESY STANLEY FORMAN)

Boston Globe, *April 6, 1976* (BOSTON PUBLIC LIBRARY)

as the darkness of the building on one side gives way to brightness on the other. It also takes us from the darkness of the foreground to the light of the background, the sun bouncing off of the windows at the center rear.

The visual textures that give the image such power are not only black and white but geometric as well. The cobblestone pavement provides strong vertical lines that direct our eyes from foreground to middle ground, where the horizontal action is taking place. The stones provide a grid, a field of action on which the incident rages. Our eyes follow the lines back, through a corridor bordered by the granite blocks of the building on the left and the alabaster white of the building on the right. The two buildings create parallel lines that help give the photograph depth and exaggerate the feeling of confinement and claustrophobia. There is no escape to the rear, which carries the viewer back into Boston's past, to the Old State House, whose Georgian facade sits bathed in sunlight.

Ahead, the direction toward which Landsmark struggles, the lane opens up onto City Hall Plaza. Built between 1963 and 1968 as part of an urban renewal program, and in an attempt to centralize government services, the plaza from the start was ridiculed and reviled. Indeed, the Project for Public Spaces placed it at the top of its list of the worst squares and plazas in the world. (Place de la Concorde in Paris and the United Nations Plaza in San Francisco rank second and third.) The spaces between the buildings are vast, the plaza seems shapeless, and the complex is cut off from any of the surrounding attractions such as Faneuil Hall and Quincy Market. Indeed, City Hall Plaza seems to have been completed with an eye toward creating a public space that impeded the possibilities for protest.

Just as space is critical to an understanding of the photograph, so is time. Not so much the time of day, though the bright light of an early April morning illuminates the scene, but historic time, which we are reminded of precisely because of where the light is hitting brightest: in the rear, on the Old State House. According to the Bostonian Society, the Old State House is the oldest surviving public building in Boston. Built in 1713, it housed the government offices of the Massachusetts Bay Colony, the council chamber of the royal governor, and the meeting place for the Massachusetts Assembly, as well as the Suffolk County courts and the Massachusetts Supreme Judicial Court. Only in 1798, with the opening of a new statehouse on Beacon Hill, did the building cease being used by state officials.

The building is most notable for another reason, and that reason is important to a reading of Forman's photograph. We carry historical and visual memories and associations to every image that we see. Sometimes we are conscious of those associations, as might be the photographer who plays off of them. For example, when Gordon Parks posed Ella Watson in front of an American flag, he relied on viewers' knowing Grant Wood's *American Gothic*, which had already become a visual icon in American culture. More frequently, it is not that we are conscious of a specific connection but that the composition of any one image suggests the forms, positions, and expressions of others, and those associations deepen the reading of any single picture.

The event and image that *The Soiling of Old Glory* brings readily to mind are the Boston Massacre and Paul Revere's engraving of the scene. On the evening of March 5, 1770, following an altercation between an apprentice and a British sentry, a crowd gathered by the

Gordon Parks, Washington D.C. Government Charwoman [Ella Watson], *1942* (LIBRARY OF CONGRESS)

customs house and began taunting a group of soldiers. The British army had been in Boston for nearly eighteen months, sent to maintain order following protests against various parliamentary acts. The crowd heckled the soldiers and threw icy snowballs at them. The soldiers, led by Captain Thomas Preston, tried to disperse the throng. Tensions mounted. With bayonets fixed, the soldiers prodded the crowd. And then the British soldiers opened fire. Several died on the spot; others succumbed later.

Three weeks later, Revere advertised for sale his broadside *The Bloody Massacre Perpetrated in King-Street.* Primarily a master sil-

Paul Revere, The Bloody Massacre Perpetrated in King-Street Boston
on March 5th, 1770, *1770* (AMERICAN ANTIQUARIAN SOCIETY)

versmith, Revere also worked as a copper plate engraver, creating illustrations for books and magazines. His depiction of the massacre is one of the most famous prints in American history, a piece of political propaganda that fueled anti-British sentiment. Revere stole the design from the artist Henry Pelham, who was not at all happy about the engraver's thievery. Pelham wrote Revere, "I thought it impossible as I knew you was not capable of doing it unless you copied it from mine and as I thought I had entrusted it in the hands of a person who had more regard to the dictates of Honour and Justice."

Within five years, Pelham would return to England, a loyalist, and Revere would take the ride that, in time, transformed him into a folk hero. Revere's print would find its way into the homes of colonists, who often paid extra to have it hand-colored. His broadside dramatizes the event, making the soldiers more orderly and organized than they were, depicting the crowd as passive, using words (the customs house is labeled "Butcher's Hall") to drive home his message. We feel enclosed in the same space as the protesters and soldiers. Our eye follows the volley, and we mourn the fallen along with the shawled woman at the center of the crowd.

The connections, both historical and visual, between Paul Revere's engraving and Stanley Forman's photograph are striking. The assault upon Landsmark took place in the literal shadows of the site of the Boston Massacre; the Old State House is the background in Revere's engraving as in Forman's photograph. Both images feature enclosed, claustrophobic spaces, and architectural shapes and textures, that create depth and confine the action. Both provide strong horizontal lines to guide the eye. In both images, the balance of light and dark, even in the colored versions of Revere's print, add drama to the scene. That the assault on Landsmark took place in 1976, as the city was preparing for the summer Bicentennial celebration, only adds to the resonance between the two images.

At a different level, so too does the story of Crispus Attucks, the black man considered the first victim of the Boston Massacre. Attucks was a runaway servant, a sailor and ropemaker in his forties who was a familiar figure among the working class of Boston. John Adams, who defended the British soldiers at their trial, identified the protesters as "a motley rabble of saucy boys, negroes and mollatoes, Irish teagues and outlandish jack tars," and he identified Attucks as an instigator who grabbed a soldier's bayonet and struck a blow. But most patriots in Boston treated him as a martyr in the cause of liberty, and he was buried in hallowed soil at the Granary Burying Ground.

Only in the mid-nineteenth century did Attucks become fully transformed into a black Revolutionary hero, a symbol not simply of liberty but of the abolition of slavery. His resurrection came at the hands of William Cooper Nell, a black Boston historian who in 1855 published *Colored Patriots of the American Revolution*. Nell opened the book with a chapter on Attucks and a renewed call for a monument to the fallen hero. Boston's black community embraced the cause, and on March 5, 1858, a year after the Dred Scott decision, which ruled blacks were not citizens, held a Crispus Attucks Day. By then, an artist had reimagined Revere's version of the Boston Massacre, which did not indicate race, and made Attucks the central figure. In the lithograph, Attucks is falling backward, his hand on the bayonet that has just pierced him.

Boston Massacre, March 5th, 1770, *1856* (AMERICAN ANTIQUARIAN SOCIETY)

The visual parallels between Forman's photograph and the print from more than a hundred years earlier are remarkable. In the aftermath of the assault on Landsmark, the connection to Crispus Attucks was not lost on writers. Editors at *Ebony* offered a blues verse:

If you see Crispus Attucks and the blacks who died to make us free
If you see Crispus Attucks and the blacks who died to make us free
Tell 'em it's business as usual in Boston and the land of liberty.

The editors wondered "what Crispus Attucks, the black who became the first martyr of the Revolution and the hero of the Boston

Massacre, would have thought of . . . [the assault on Landsmark]. He would have understood the racism, of course, for all or almost all of the white Founding Fathers were marked by the racism of their time. But it is doubtful he would have understood the insensitivity of public officials who are repeating the mistakes of the white Founding Fathers and subtly fanning the flames of discord with code words like 'forced busing' . . . Haven't we learned in all these years that there can be no salvation for us, either in time or eternity, if we do not regain the sense and the spirit of the revolutionary dream proclaimed on July 4, 1776?"

A letter to the *Boston Globe* noted that "it is ironic that Mr. Landsmark was attacked within a stonethrow's [*sic*] distance of the site of the Boston Massacre, where Crispus Attucks, a black man, was the first person to die in the American Revolution. Now, as evidenced by this attack, the black people of Boston have very little reason to celebrate the Bicentennial, for they still are not free to safely walk the streets of this city."

Landsmark himself also suggested the connection. At a press conference held on April 7, 1976, he pointed out to a reporter, according to the black newspaper the *Bay State Banner*, "that he was struck in the face with an American flag in front of City Hall not far from Faneuil Hall (a so-called 'cradle of liberty' where the American Revolutionaries used to gather), during the Bicentennial year, at a location not far from the site 'where Crispus Attucks . . . got his.'"

Paul Revere's engraving of the Boston Massacre, Crispus Attucks, and the Revolutionary tradition are not the only deep context for reading *The Soiling of Old Glory*. Forman's photograph also evoked visual and historical connections to another image forever tied to the story of freedom: Joe Rosenthal's photograph of the flag

raising on Mt. Suribachi on February 23, 1945. One writer to the
Herald American thought that the photograph "of the young man
lunging at the struggling Mr. Landsmark's face with the steel-
shafted American flag—this picture was historic. Doesn't it remind
you somehow of that oldie of the Marines raising the flag on Iwo
Jima?"

Rosenthal's photograph is probably the most famous and most
widely reproduced image in history. It appeared in newspapers
throughout the world, was used in a poster campaign for a War Loan
Drive, was placed on a postage stamp, and served as the model for
the Marine Corps War Memorial. It received the Pulitzer Prize. It
also proved controversial. Throughout his life, Rosenthal was forced
to defend its authenticity against accusations that he staged the
scene.

Joe Rosenthal, born in 1911, became a newspaper photographer
in the early 1930s. His poor eyesight kept him from enlisting as a
soldier, but it did not prevent him from serving as a combat photographer for the Associated Press. He was always at the front line of
the action, whether crossing the Atlantic in a convoy or diving with
navy bombers. He was among the initial wave of marines who hit
the beaches at Iwo Jima. He later discussed the impossibility of the
situation. "No man who survived the beach can tell you how he did
it," Rosenthal recalled. "It was like walking through rain and not
getting wet."

The battle for Iwo Jima took thirty-six days and left more than
twenty-five thousand American soldiers dead or wounded. On the
fifth day, the marines reached the top of Mt. Suribachi, located on
the southern end of the island. Rosenthal and his Speed Graphic
camera were not far behind. On his way up the mountain on the

morning of February 23, accompanied by two other journalists, Rosenthal encountered several marines on their way down. Lou Lowery, another photographer, said that the soldiers had already raised the flag. Indeed, Lowery had gotten the shot at around ten thirty. Rosenthal went to the peak anyhow. When he got there, there was a group of marines arranging a second flag raising. Bob Campbell, one of the photographers with Rosenthal, took a picture of the first flag coming down as the second went up.

Rosenthal backed up to get the picture of the second flag raising. Where he stood, he recalled, "the ground sloped down toward the center of the volcanic crater, and I found that the ground line was in my way. I put my Speed Graphic down and quickly piled up some stones and a Jap sandbag to raise me about two feet (I am only 5 feet 5 inches tall) and I picked up the camera and climbed up on the pile. I decided on a lens setting between f-8 and f-11, and set the speed at 1-400th of a second." Bill Genaust, a marine photographer shooting motion picture footage, was next to Rosenthal and asked if he was in his way. Rosenthal said no, and as he answered, the men lifted the pole and he took the photograph.

He had no idea whether the picture was any good, and he also took a posed shot of all the marines together in front of the flag. This second picture, along with the fact of the two flag raisings, led a *Time-Life* correspondent to report that Rosenthal's photo of the flag raising was staged. The reporter retracted the story, but the damage was done, and Rosenthal continually had to defend the photograph and retell the story of how it came to be.

One reason for the persistence of the accusation is the brilliance of the image. It is hard to believe that a photograph this perfect was not posed. The six men (yes, six; two stand behind) are

Joe Rosenthal, Flag Raising on Mt. Suribachi, *1945* (LIBRARY OF CONGRESS)

united, their exertions a ballet of form and effort. Notice the bend in the right leg of each man. We do not see their faces, just their bodies and their hands. Their anonymity makes their effort that much more noble. The last soldier in the line is forever striving upward, forever trying to raise the flag, forever trying to close the gap between reach and reward. At their feet is the chaos of debris that contrasts with the serenity of the valley and horizon below. The powerful diagonal of the hundred-pound pole slashes across empty gray sky. The flag itself, mirroring the postures of the men, prepares to unfurl.

For a generation, Rosenthal's photograph reigned as the ultimate symbol of American sacrifice and patriotism. Forman's picture stood immediately as the antithesis to Rosenthal's, an image that captured how far the United States had fallen since the heady days of 1945, a picture of national hatred that literally desecrated the achievement and memory of the men on Mt. Suribachi. Senator Edward Kennedy, for one, immediately made the connection. In the two years since busing had started, Kennedy had personally experienced the rage of the crowd that denounced him for his support of Judge Garrity and the court's order. "There are two pictures in which the American flag has appeared that have made the most powerful impact on me," he said. "The first was that of Iwo Jima in World War II. The second was that shown here in Massachusetts two weeks ago in which the American flag appeared to have been used in the attempted garroting of an individual solely on the basis of his color. That's been obviously one of the most moving and shocking actions that any of us could imagine."

It seemed as if one could write a history of the nation's decline in the thirty-one years between photographs. Not merely the busing crisis but a general sense of malaise afflicted the country in the mid-1970s. Whatever economic and social progress had been made in the 1950s and '60s seemed stalled. Americans suffered through Vietnam and they suffered through Watergate, two crises that raised fundamental questions about patriotism and the vitality of the nation. People felt lost, and into that sense of dislocation entered Forman's shocking photograph that seemed to confirm the worst nightmares over the fate of the country.

It was not only a matter of patriotism but also one of faith. If visually *The Soiling of Old Glory* could be tied to the Revolutionary War and World War II, it could also be tied to religious images of crucifixion. The iconography of crucifixion, like that of Madonna and child, is so deeply embedded in the visual culture of the Western world that it sometimes seems as if any image can be made to fit the profile. In *The Soiling of Old Glory*, the religious symbolism is apparent. The assault occurred on April 5, during the Lenten season, and one writer to the *Herald American* reminded readers that "Easter is coming and with it, we are taught, hope and joy. May we dare hope that Mr. Landsmark and other innocent victims of similar unprovoked attacks search their hearts for charity towards those people and say 'Forgive them Father, for they know not what they are doing.'"

Landsmark's outstretched arm and bent body evoke images of Christ on the cross. More specifically, Joseph Rakes's use of the flag as a spear suggests the stabbing of Christ in the side by the Roman soldier Longinus, who afterward converted to Christianity and was canonized. Representations of the Crucifixion often included the piercing of Christ. One example should suffice to demonstrate how Forman's photograph suggested the scene of the Crucifixion. Peter Paul Rubens, the Flemish artist, painted *Christ on the Cross* sometime around 1620. In the painting, Longinus, dressed in black, is about to drive the spear into Christ's side. The space is tight and crowded. We read the painting from left to right, and we too, like the observer in the foreground right, wish to turn away in mourning for what we see.

Reading *The Soiling of Old Glory* in the light of Paul Revere's engraving, Joe Rosenthal's photograph, and Peter Paul Rubens's painting deepens our understanding of Forman's accomplishment

Peter Paul Rubens, Christ on the Cross, *1620* (VIAMSE MUSEA)

and demonstrates why his photograph might be considered a visual masterpiece as much as a striking example of spot news journalism. The image comes into even sharper focus if we examine it in the context of the other pictures Forman took at the rally. Doing so provides a fuller portrait of the assault and reveals ways in which the photograph has been misread.

Forman took twenty-three pictures at the rally, seventeen with the 20 mm lens, all of which depict the assault, and six with the other camera that had the 35 mm lens. The first photograph, slightly out of

Stanley Forman, contact sheet, 1976 (COURTESY STANLEY FORMAN)

focus, captures the assault just under way. Whatever expletives have been shouted echo in the air, and the protesters seem to descend on Landsmark and another black man, both of whom are in defensive postures. The youths circle, fists cocked. The flag bearer is to the side, with the other marchers.

With the second shot, Forman has found his focus. The confrontation has drawn the attention of all the spectators. Those who have already walked past look back. The flag holder has his eyes set on the scene. In the next shot, Landsmark recoils from an outstretched fist. All eyes are on the punch. The youth in leather jacket and white pants is preparing to attack. A boy to his side stands on his toes, straining to see the fight. Toward the rear, a man with coat and tie seems to be rushing toward the scene, but he is not racing in to break it up. He is a news photographer, caught in front of the procession, rushing back to try to get a picture.

In photographs four through seven, the assault continues. The student in white pants gets his blows in as Landsmark covers up. The boy who was on his toes now races in and kicks Landsmark. The other black man shields himself and moves away. The presence of the foreground youth, hands in pockets, would seem not to bode well for either man, but he cuts through the plane of Forman's camera, and it looks for a moment as if both men will manage to flee the assault. But others are rushing in, as the next two photographs make clear. The boy in the plaid shirt has made his way back to Landsmark, followed by a student in a white jacket. The other victim will make his escape, but Landsmark is caught. The photographer in the rear is still out of range, camera in hand.

With the tenth shot, Forman felt the motor drive failing. The negative reveals problems with the film, and the next shots are double-exposed. *Herald* editors cropped out the double-exposed portion of one of these images and placed it on the front page below the assault with the flag. Between double-exposed and torn negatives there is a clear shot of the assault. This is an effective spot news photograph in its own right. The angle is low, giving the feeling of being on the ground and in the fray. The scene is open, a horizontal triangle of action in which the fallen Landsmark is at the pinnacle. To the left, the flag swirls into action. The figure who earlier had been in the foreground has moved to the far left, staying out of trouble. To the right, a mustachioed man in a windbreaker is the only figure in action, racing to the scene. In the background center left, a woman holds her hands to her face. She is reminiscent of the shawled woman in a similar location in Paul Revere's print, modeling the viewer's shock.

Forman switched to manual, and the very next shot made headlines. As the contact sheet makes clear, the original shot was cropped to create a more dramatic picture. The open space to the right alters the gravity of the image, making it feel less claustrophobic. The *Herald American* image is cropped on top and bottom as well, compressing the action and bringing into greater prominence the Old State House by reducing the building and sky behind. The wider panoramic view does not work nearly as well as the tight focus on the flag and Landsmark.

Ever since there have been negatives, documentary and news photographers have cropped the pictures they have taken. A well-cropped photograph eliminates unnecessary or irrelevant pictorial information, brings out the aesthetic value of the shot, and helps to focus the essential story. The practice is commonplace and bears comparison to quoting only the essential part of a speech. As long as

the central meaning of the image or text is not altered, a cropped photograph is every bit as objective a document as an uncropped one, even though it undoubtedly alters the dimensions of the story presented to the viewer.

In many respects, the uncropped and cropped versions of *The Soiling of Old Glory* stand as a testimony to the effective use of the technique. At the same time, all photographs now carry with them some suspicion that they misrepresent reality. The anxiety developed alongside the form itself and grew out of the opposite assumption that governed ideas about photographs in the beginning. In the first half of the nineteenth century, viewers believed that daguerreotypes were perfect representations of objects in nature, providing exact depictions of what they recorded. These "sun pictures," as they were

sometimes called, were but "pencils of nature." Many went so far as
to believe that photographs captured not only external facts but internal truths as well. A portrait was said to reveal a person's soul.
Ralph Waldo Emerson, the philosopher of American individualism,
agreed: "The Daguerreotype is good for its authenticity. No man
quarrels with his shadow, nor will he with his miniature when the
sun was the painter. Here is no interference, and the distortions are
not blunders of an artist, but only those of motion, imperfect light,
and the like." Unfortunately for Emerson, he despaired over his ap-
pearance in daguerreotypes and lamented the "assinizing" effect the
camera had on him.

Assumptions about the objectivity of photographs remain part
of our belief system, long after photographers realized they were not

simply machine operators but artists who simultaneously captured and manipulated the scene before them in both subtle and overt ways. Lewis Hine, whose portraits of workers shaped Progressive Era cries for social justice, said it best: "While photographs may not lie, liars may photograph. It becomes necessary then to see to it that the camera we depend on contracts no bad habits." The worst habits of photographers, those that played off of viewers' assumptions about photographs as documents of reality, involved directly manipulating the scene being photographed. One of the early examples of this transgression came during the Civil War when Alexander Gardner, eager to communicate to viewers a message about the war, moved a dead soldier at Gettysburg to a spot between some rocks, propped his rifle up, and took a picture titled *Home of a Rebel Sharpshooter.*

Overt acts of manipulation are unusual, and even subtle ones that involve actions other than photographic processes are not tolerated. For example, in 1936, Arthur Rothstein, a documentary photographer for the Farm Security Administration, found a cow's skull in the badlands of South Dakota. The skull, resting atop parched, cracked earth, became a symbol of drought and depression. But it was soon discovered that Rothstein moved the skull some ten feet closer to the cactus for the purposes of composing a better image. Opponents of Roosevelt's New Deal denounced Rothstein's photograph as propaganda and used it to condemn FDR's policies.

As viewers, we continue to bounce between the extremes of seeing photographs as objective representations of fact and seeing them as artistic constructions that create and interpret reality rather than record it. We will not tolerate overt acts of manipulation, nor should we. Composed and contrived photographs are lies that may get at some form of emotional truth but cannot serve the demands of documentary truth. At the same time, we tolerate certain photographic practices and techniques such as cropping or adjusting contrast, and we should. These techniques, as long as they do not alter the content of the image, are tools that make for a clearer, more focused photograph. The technique is not entirely innocent, and it does serve as an important reminder that the photographer is no neutral spectator. But when *The Soiling of Old Glory* was cropped, editors created a more powerful image, not one that distorted the truth of the moment.

It is possible, however, that an even deeper truth resides in the multiple-exposed image that immediately preceded the front page shot that went on to a win a Pulitzer Prize. That image captures the frenzy and uncertainty of the assault, the blur that was the event. The other images advance frame by frame; each is a tableau that we study before moving on to see what happens next. But in this picture, linearity gives way. The flag bearer is both racing in on the left and swinging the flag at the center. Landsmark is both being beaten to the ground and being lifted up. The picture matches the blurriness of the event, how it must have looked from the point of view of the victim: fist, flag, frenzy. And the multiple exposures provide something else as well: the tear in the negative reminds us that the technology of representation is inseparable from our understanding of the event itself, that a photographer is present. Here, then, is a pictorial truth that the camera can provide.

A question that remains in viewing *The Soiling of Old Glory* is whether our perception of what is taking place in the photograph accurately reflects what is indeed occurring. Photos deceive sometimes not because of the designs of the photographer but because the viewer

Alfred Stieglitz, Steerage, *1907* (LIBRARY OF CONGRESS)

does not have complete information. Take, for example, Alfred Stieglitz's *Steerage.* Stieglitz was among the first to elevate photography to
the realm of art. *Steerage* certainly stands as a striking modernist
work, with lines and shapes and depths that suggest an artistic composition. The photograph is also a document, one that represents class
distinctions and the plight of the immigrant at the turn of the twentieth century. For years, I thought of the photograph as a stunning
depiction of the journey to Ellis Island. And then I learned that the
ship on which Stieglitz took the picture was not arriving but leaving,
bound for Europe. These poor and huddled masses are not seeking a

new life in America but are returning home. The photograph remains a powerful image of migration, but any reading of the picture that does not consider the contextual fact that the ship is departing, not arriving, is fatally flawed.

There is also the problem of sequence in considering photographic truth. The camera freezes time, giving us always a moment, a fraction of a narrative that stretches before and after the isolated instant. The question is whether the frozen moment tricks the eye, leading the viewer to one interpretation whereas another, or opposite, interpretation would be closer to the truth of the event. Consider the controversy over a photograph taken on 9/11 but not published until 2006 because of how disturbing it seemed.

On the morning of 9/11, Thomas Hoepker, an experienced photojournalist, crossed over from Manhattan into Queens and Brooklyn in an attempt to get closer to the scene of the catastrophe. He stopped his car in Williamsburg to shoot a group of young people sitting by the waterfront with the plume of smoke rising from across the river. He did not publish the shot at the time, feeling it was "ambiguous and confusing," a pastoral scene of five youths chatting amicably as the towers burned.

David Friend included the image in *Watching the World Change: The Stories Behind the Images of 9/11.* In the book, Hoepker expresses his concern that the youths in the photograph "didn't seem to care." Seizing upon this, Frank Rich, in his column in the *New York Times* as the fifth anniversary approached, saw the photograph as a prescient symbol of indifference and amnesia. He characterized the New Yorkers as "enjoying the radiant late-summer sun and chatting away." "The young people in Mr. Hoepker's photo," Rich wrote, "aren't necessarily callous. They're just American."

Thomas Hoepker, Young People on the Brooklyn Waterfront, September
II, 200I (MAGNUM PHOTOS)

David Plotz, of the online magazine *Slate,* would have none of
this interpretation. "Those New Yorkers Weren't Relaxing," the
headline argued. "The subjects," Plotz observed, "have looked away
from the towers for a moment not because they're bored with 9/11,
but because they're citizens participating in the most important act
in a democracy—civic debate." Plotz argued that Rich took a "cheap
shot" in exploiting as metaphor the image of citizens turning their
backs on the conflagration, and he called for a response from any of
the subjects.

Shortly thereafter, Walter Sipser wrote to Plotz: "It's Me in That
9/11 Photo." He said, "We were in a profound state of shock and disbelief, like everyone else we encountered that day." Sipser denounced

Hoepker for not trying to ascertain the state of mind of the photo's subjects and for perpetuating a misinterpretation of a frozen moment.

Hoepker responded that "the image has touched many people exactly because it remains fuzzy and ambiguous in all its sun-drenched sharpness," especially five years after the event. And he wondered: was the picture "just the devious lie of a snapshot, which ignored the seconds before and after I had clicked the shutter?"

"The devious lie of a snapshot" is a marvelous phrase. It is not the photographer who is devious but the nature of the snapshot itself, which isolates and freezes action, disconnecting it from context and sequence. More often than not, the single frame is true to the event as recorded in the frames that come before and after. But every so often, as in the case of *Young People on the Brooklyn Waterfront, September 11, 2001*, the single shot can distort our understanding of what is taking place. Such is the situation with *The Soiling of Old Glory*.

There are two ways in which *The Soiling of Old Glory* tricks the eye. The first concerns the flag. The day after the assault, the *Globe* reported that "news pictures indicated that the staff of an American flag was used in the attack." It looks as if Rakes is taking dead aim at Landsmark's body and is preparing to plunge the staff of the flag into him. But as the double-exposed previous picture makes clear, Rakes is swinging, not driving, the flag toward his victim. *The Soiling of Old Glory* freezes the flag in its movement from side to side, giving the impression that the flag bearer is thrusting Old Glory into Landsmark. In fact, the staff of the flag missed its victim, though early reports claimed that Landsmark had been hit by it. Knowing this takes little away from the power and meaning

of the image—Landsmark was indeed assaulted with the American flag—but it does illustrate how a photograph can suggest a story that is not quite right.

Perhaps more significant is the second way in which the photograph is misread. The man who, in a previous image, is in motion racing to the scene has arrived and is grabbing Landsmark. It would appear that he has joined the fray to get in his punches and, worse yet, is pinioning Landsmark's arms so that the flag bearer has a clear line of attack. In fact, the person holding Landsmark is Jim Kelly, one of the adult organizers of the protest, and he has raced in not to bind Landsmark but to save him from further violence. Kelly was helping Landsmark to his feet—recall that he had been on all fours a few seconds before. As the president of the South Boston Information Center and a ringleader of the protests, Kelly felt responsible for

Stanley Forman shooting the scene, 1976 (COURTESY STANLEY FORMAN)

the actions of the teenagers, and he dashed in to try to break up the fight. In another photograph taken a moment later (see facing page), he can be seen holding his arms out wide trying to keep the protesters back as Landsmark stumbles to safety.

Kelly was a vocal, visible, militant opponent of busing, but he did not condone violence. His effort to come to Landsmark's aid is a noteworthy act, and our knowledge of it changes our understanding of the photograph. The assault on Landsmark was brutal and vicious, and Forman's photograph captured the truth of the moment, the toxic cocktail of racial hatred and patriotic fervor that stunned Boston and the nation. It turns out it captured something else as well, only no one knew it at the time. A white man is coming to the aid of a black man. Perhaps there was some hope for Boston on the vexed subject of race. As it turns out, both Landsmark and Kelly would play key roles in shaping the future. As a photojournalist, Forman would too.

There is a picture of him taking the shot. An Associated Press photographer covering the incident has inadvertently caught Forman in the frame. Forman's body is hunched and taut as he snaps away. Landsmark is trying to flee, but a student has hold of his coat and is preparing to punch him. Landsmark's satchel lies by his feet on the ground. Rakes and the flag circle toward the victim in the background; Kelly moves toward him in the foreground. There is space for Landsmark to run, if only he can slip loose. He strains in the direction of Forman. Afterward, Landsmark would wonder why no one came to his aid. But Forman is there, with his finger on the shutter.

CHAPTER 4

OLD GLORY

WHEN BOSTON BID to host the 2004 Democratic National Convention, one of Mayor Thomas Menino's goals was to change the perception of the city. "For too many people around the country," he declared, "when they think of Boston the image they remember is of Ted Landsmark getting hit with an American flag. I wanted the opportunity to show people we are a much different city now, a city where diversity is welcome." John Kerry, the Democratic nominee for president, had his own reasons to talk about the flag, and in his acceptance speech at the Democratic National Convention in Boston in the summer of 2004, he waxed eloquent: "You see that flag up there. We call her Old Glory. The stars and stripes forever. I fought under that flag, as did so many of you here and all across our country . . . For us, that flag is the most powerful symbol of who we are and what we believe in. Our strength. Our diversity. Our love of country. All that makes America both great and good."

The cult of the American flag of which Kerry spoke took root in the Civil War. The Continental Congress may have created the flag in 1777, and Francis Scott Key may have celebrated it in verse in 1814, but during the Civil War the flag transcended its status as a marker of sovereignty. It became a symbol of the meaning of the nation, and the cloth itself became cause for devotion.

A sermon delivered by Henry Ward Beecher in May 1861 set the tone for the new understanding. The son of Lyman Beecher, one of the leading evangelical ministers of the day, and the brother of Harriet Beecher Stowe, whose novel *Uncle Tom's Cabin* was outsold only by the Bible, Beecher had a national reputation as a fiery orator and proponent of social reform. His pulpit was the Plymouth Church in Brooklyn, New York, and on this spring day he addressed two companies of the Brooklyn Fourteenth Regiment on "The National Flag."

"A thoughtful mind," Beecher observed, "when it sees a nation's flag, sees not the flag, but the nation itself. And whatever may be its symbols, its insignia, he reads chiefly in the flag the government, the principles, the truths, the history, that belong to the nation that sets it forth." He declared "this glorious National Flag" to be "the Flag of Liberty" and lamented that "this flag should, in our own nation, and by our own people, be spit upon, and trampled under foot."

Beecher perhaps had not yet heard the appellation, but his use of *glorious* captured something in the air: the Civil War gave Old Glory its name. No less a writer than Nathaniel Hawthorne picked up on the new phrase. Hawthorne had returned to the United States in 1860, after several years' absence. The outbreak of the war reinvigorated the fifty-seven-year-old novelist: following a tour of Washington and the surrounding area, he returned home to Concord and in April 1862 wrote "Chiefly About War-Matters" for the *Atlantic Monthly*. Hawthorne was no zealous Union man, and the dedication of his final book to his friend Franklin Pierce, the former Democratic president who during the war denounced the abolitionists, brought condemnation. In his essay, signed "A Peaceable Man," Hawthorne analyzed "the anomaly of two allegiances," the one to the State and the other to the Nation. The State was represented by "the altar and the hearth," whereas the Nation "has no symbol but a flag."

That flag, he observed, was everywhere: "The waters around Fortress Monroe were thronged with a gallant array of ships of war and transports, wearing the Union flag,—'Old Glory,' as I hear it called these days." In their diaries and memoirs, Union soldiers also started using the phrase. In January 1862, David Day gazed on "'old glory' proudly waving over the frowning battlements at Fortress Monroe." Two months later, George Smith noted that "when Old Glory crept up to the masthead in the morning and unfolded in the breeze he was greeted with the cannon's roar." In his memoir, George Sherman could not express his feelings as he returned north at the end of the war and "beheld in the distance 'Old Glory' as we had become accustomed to call it."

Feelings for the flag were already running high when the *New York Herald* reported a scene that took place in Nashville in February 1862. Union soldiers had taken the city, and "an aged gentleman, a native of Salem, Massachusetts, and for twenty-eight years a citizen of Nashville, came through the crowd to the colonel and produced an American flag, thirty-eight by nineteen feet in size." This was Captain William Driver, a retired New England sea captain. The flag that he provided had been given to him in 1824, a twenty-first-birthday present and a gift as he took command of the 110-ton brig *Charles Doggett* in Salem harbor. Legend has it that as the flag unfurled he remarked, "God bless you. I'll call it 'Old Glory.'"

Driver retired in 1837 from a career at sea that included making at least two trips around the world and taking the descendants of sailors who had mutinied on the *Bounty* in 1789 from Tahiti to Pitcairn Island. He settled in Nashville, to be near his brothers, and remarried after the death of his wife. Through it all, he was never without his flag, Old Glory, which he flew on all occasions.

When secession came, and Confederates tried to confiscate the flag, Driver had it updated (from twenty-four to thirty-four stars) and sewn inside a comforter. On February 25, the Sixth Ohio Regiment entered the city and hoisted a flag over the statehouse. Driver ran to retrieve his flag. He wrote to his daughter that he "carried our flag—Old Glory as we have been used to call it—to the Capitol and presented it to the Ohio Sixth. I hoisted it with my own hands on the Capitol over this proud city amid the heaven-stirring cheers of thousands."

There is a flag in the Smithsonian that is said to be the original Old Glory. It has thirty-four stars and a small white anchor but is smaller than the flag reported in the newspaper in 1862. If the flag in the Smithsonian is indeed the original Old Glory, the provenance goes something like this: Driver, fearing that the winds would destroy Old Glory, substituted another flag the following day. In 1873, he gave Old Glory to his daughter, Mary Jane Driver Roland. In 1922, she presented the flag to President Warren G. Harding, who gave it to the Smithsonian Institution. A niece of Driver's, Harriet Ruth Cooke, contested this history and claimed that she had been given the original Old Glory by her uncle. If so, its whereabouts are unknown. Finally, when the Sixth Ohio Regiment left, they took a flag with them. It was probably the replacement flag that Driver provided the following day. The soldiers placed it in one of the baggage wagons. We know what happened to that flag: famished mules made a meal of it.

In the aftermath of the Civil War, the cult of the American flag intensified. Perhaps the most popular printed image of the last decades of the nineteenth century was Archibald Willard's *Yankee Doodle*, later known as *Spirit of '76*. Willard had served in the Eighty-sixth Ohio Volunteer Infantry during the war, and he began drawing military scenes. He developed a partnership with James Ryder, a photographer and businessman, and together the two did good business selling colored prints of Willard's work. One of his most popular prints, titled *Pluck*, showed a group of boys being pulled in a wagon by a dog who takes off after a passing rabbit. Willard understood well the public's preference for scenes that entertained and amused.

For the 1876 Centennial Exposition in Philadelphia, Willard painted *Yankee Doodle*. His original intent was to do a humorous picture that poked fun at small-town celebrations and what had become the annual July 4 ritual of old-timers dressing up and reenacting the Revolutionary spirit. Willard tried his hand at this, but none of the sketches worked. Ryder thought the picture should be more sober, and Willard eliminated most of the humor. The portrait of the central figure of the elderly man with the drum was based on Willard's father. The model for the fifer had served in the Civil War, and the drummer boy attended Brooks Military School in Cleveland.

The picture is well composed. Our eye goes immediately to the thirteen-star flag, upright between the center drummer and fifer. Of course, the flag, in a painting that came to be known as *Spirit of '76*, is an anachronism, as it was not adopted until 1777. The boy looks to the elderly man. All three step forward in unison, leading a few soldiers who follow, one with a cap raised in apparent celebration.

Archibald Willard, Spirit of
'76, 1876 (LIBRARY OF
CONGRESS)

According to a piece Ryder published in 1895, viewers thought of the unit as three generations of one family who have stepped forward to reconstitute a broken line (the shattered cannon) and lead the troops toward victory. In the bottom right foreground, a fallen soldier doffs his cap to the flag as it passes by.

The original painting was displayed in the annex to Memorial Hall at the Philadelphia Exposition. One newspaper critic loathed the painting: "There is a great waste of good material here, and Mr. Willard's work is rather oppressive." But what the critics thought did not matter. For the public, the painting was a sensation, and Willard and Ryder couldn't keep the chromolithograph in stock. Willard painted multiple versions, as was the custom with popular paintings. In a later rendering, the fallen soldier is sitting upright. Perhaps the depiction of a dying man saluting the flag as it passed created too much dissonance in viewers who wanted only to celebrate victory; he is cropped out entirely from the postage stamp issued by the United States Postal Service.

When Willard painted *Spirit of '76*, calls for a day to honor the flag were in the air. As early as 1861, Charles Dudley Warner, editor and writer, called in the *Hartford Press* for making June 14, the day on which the flag resolution of 1777 was adopted, a national holiday. For the hundredth anniversary of that occasion, the *New York Times* lobbied for "a general display of the American flag throughout the country." In the years that followed, cities and towns across most of the nation informally celebrated the centennial of the flag. In Phila-delphia, five hundred school children received small flags. In Wash-ington, the flag flew from all public buildings. Religious groups joined with secular to celebrate the flag. But not everyone reveled in the cult of the American flag. With the Civil War still fresh in their memory, southerners clung to their faith in the state, not the nation. An editor at the *Richmond Dispatch* thought that "patriotism must go deeper than the flying of the bunting."

Nevertheless, starting in the 1880s, momentum began to build for the establishment of a national flag day. Convention has it that Bernard Cigrand, a Wisconsin teacher, first promoted the idea in 1885, and while Cigrand certainly published essays and editorials re-minding readers of the importance of June 14, few Americans needed his coaxing to celebrate the day. Flag celebration seemed everywhere, and soon school superintendents and state governors issued proclama-tions of commemoration for the flag. By 1898, a writer for an evan-gelical newspaper lent support to celebrations of the flag, especially in the context of war with Spain, and pointed out that "June 14th has come to be largely considered by the patriotic citizens of this country as 'Flag Day.'" So widespread was reverence for the flag, the *Advocate of Peace* offered readers a reminder that "there was a time when banners and flags . . . were unquestionably symbols of hatred, strife and war." In an article called "Worship of the Flag," the writer asked, "Is there no higher idea of a flag?' and answered that flags must be transformed into symbols of peace: "As they have been made the means of unifying the national life in conquest and hatred and destruction, they must be made to serve as means of unifying it in the means of carrying out the deeper and noble purposes for which nations are called into being."

The author's dream of making the American flag "a flag of peace" did not come to pass, and with World War I the flag again traveled overseas in support of what Woodrow Wilson hoped would be a world "made safe for democracy." Less than a year before asking for a declaration of war, President Wilson issued a presidential proclamation on May 30, 1916, that established June 14 as Flag Day. Several decades later, on August 3, 1949, in the aftermath of another war, President Harry S. Truman signed into law a congressional act designating a National Flag Day.

Even as the flag came to be venerated in the late nineteenth and early twentieth centuries, it became subject to another kind of treatment: desecration. Of course, it makes perfect sense that the two might emerge side by side, an object worshipped and reviled, an icon and a target. Reports and pamphlets in support of legislation against federal flag desecration began to appear, primarily in response not to overt acts of destruction but to the commercial use of the image of the flag. Arguing that "old glory is too sacred a symbol to be misused by any party, creed, or faction," one writer included a list of objects on which "old glory . . . is treated with grave disrespect or used for mercenary purposes." The items ranged from pocket handkerchiefs and doormats to lemon wrappers and whiskey bottles. In 1890, the House Judiciary Committee recommended passage of a law that made it a misdemeanor to "use the national flag, either by printing, painting, or affixing said flag, or otherwise attaching to the same any advertisement for public display, or private gain."

By 1898, the American Flag Association had been formed, and the anxiety over mistreatment of the flag had shifted from commercial misuse to physical destruction. "It should hardly be a question for argument whether a man may wantonly and maliciously tear our country's flag to shreds or trample it into the mire," claimed a petition to Congress submitted by the Milwaukee Daughters of the American Revolution. In speech after speech, Charles Kingsbury Miller, a retired Illinois newspaper executive, called for legislation protecting the flag, a "sacred jewel" that commanded "national reverence." The social anxieties that animated Miller's campaign included the fear of immigrants ("the multitude of uneducated foreigners who land upon our friendly shores") and socialist anarchy ("the red flag of danger flies in America"). In response, state legislatures began to adopt flag-desecration statutes that prohibited using the flag for commercial purposes, placing any markings upon it, or publicly defacing or defiling the flag by words or actions.

These state laws were challenged in the courts by businesses that used the flag for advertising purposes and had been convicted and fined. In 1900, the Illinois Supreme Court ruled the state law unconstitutional on the grounds that it violated the Fourteenth Amendment provision that forbids states from abridging a citizen's

privileges and immunities. In 1907, the question of the constitutionality of a Nebraska law wound its way to the U.S. Supreme Court.
The law, passed in 1903, made it a misdemeanor "for anyone to sell,
expose for sale, or have in possession for sale, any article of merchan-
dise upon which shall have been printed or placed, for purposes of
advertisement, a representation of the flag of the United States." In
Halter v. Nebraska, the plaintiffs, convicted under the state law of
bottling beer with an image of the American flag on the label, ap-
pealed on the grounds that the statute infringed on their liberties as
guaranteed by the Fourteenth Amendment.

In an 8–1 decision, the Court upheld the Nebraska law. Justice
John Marshall Harlan, whom history would honor for his vigorous
dissent in *Plessy v. Ferguson* (1896)—"our Constitution is color-
blind"—delivered the opinion. Guided by the constitutional principle that states have the power to legislate as long as the legislation
does not manifestly violate the Constitution, Harlan held that the
Nebraska law did not infringe upon any constitutionally protected
rights. Where Congress has not legislated, the states still could. "By
the statute in question," Harlan ruled, "the state has in substance
declared that no one subject to its jurisdiction shall use the flag for
purposes of trade and traffic, a purpose wholly foreign to that for
which it was provided by the nation. Such a use tends to degrade and
cheapen the flag in the estimation of the people, as well as to defeat
the object of maintaining it as an emblem of national power and
national honor. And we cannot hold that any privilege of American
citizenship or that any right of personal liberty is violated by a state
enactment forbidding the flag to be used as an advertisement on a
bottle of beer."

In short order, uneasiness over the commercial exploitation of the flag subsided as American consumer culture accelerated. Of far greater concern were acts of defiling the flag, especially through burning. The tension between flag mania and flag protest reached one pinnacle during World War I. In June 1916, in New York, Bouck White, a Harvard-educated Congregational minister who fused Christianity and socialism in forming the Church of the Social Revolution, was convicted of burning an American flag that also bore the symbols of other nations. He was fined and sentenced to thirty days and told by the judge, "If ever was a time in this great Republic when every American should be true and loyal to the flag, it is now."

As far as we know, none of those prosecuted for burning the flag as a protest against American involvement in World War I, or as an expression of political dissent, raised the issue that would certainly come to dominate discussion of flag desecration in the second half of the century: the First Amendment protection of free speech. The argument would not emerge until 1931, when the Supreme Court struck down state laws that originated in postwar fear of the spread of socialism in America. In the case *Stromberg v. California*, the appellant was charged with displaying a red flag in a public place "as a sign, symbol and emblem of opposition to organized government." Writing for the majority, Chief Justice Charles Evans Hughes overturned the state conviction primarily on the grounds that the statute was vaguely constructed. Hughes did not mention the First Amendment but rather the right of free speech found in the due process clause of the Fourteenth Amendment. The state has a legitimate interest in preventing "utterances which incite to violence and crime and threaten the overthrow of organized government," but displaying a red flag is not such an utterance. In his dissent, Justice Pierce

Butler said the Court was not called upon to decide whether the display of a flag constituted speech, but it was too late: what one did to or with a flag might be seen as a form of constitutionally protected expression.

To try to codify what was considered proper treatment of the flag, Franklin Roosevelt, in the midst of World War II, signed into law the Federal Flag Code. The code, approved on June 22, 1942, provided guidelines for the proper display and use of the flag. Section 4 of the code includes the admonitions that "no disrespect should be shown to the flag; . . . the flag should not be dipped to any person or thing; . . . the flag should never be carried flat or horizontally, but always aloft and free." Section 7 of the code includes instructions on proper decorum during the Pledge of Allegiance.

The Flag Code was a guide for proper behavior. Penalties for failure to comply would have to come from legislative enactments, and the Supreme Court would play its role as the arbiter of constitutionality. In 1943, the Court heard the case of *West Virginia State Board of Education v. Barnette*, which centered on the issue of compulsory flag salute in public schools. The appellees were Jehovah's Witnesses whose religious beliefs did not permit them to salute any image or symbol, including the flag. In a 6–3 decision, the Court ruled that the state's action violated the First and Fourteenth Amendments. Justice Robert H. Jackson's majority opinion is remembered for his admonition that freedom means allowing dissent, especially in those areas that are most meaningful: "To believe that patriotism will not flourish if patriotic ceremonies are voluntary and spontaneous instead of a compulsory routine is to make an unflattering estimate of the appeal of our institutions to free minds. We can have intellectual individualism and the rich cultural diversities that we owe to exceptional minds only at the price of occasional eccentricity and abnormal attitudes. When they are so harmless to others or to the State as those we deal with here, the price is not too great. But freedom to differ is not limited to things that do not matter much. That would be a mere shadow of freedom. The test of its substance is the right to differ as to things that touch the heart of the existing order."

The Court's decisions in *Halter*, *Stromberg*, and *West Virginia Board of Education* would serve as precedent for the next string of flag-desecration cases. These would emerge out of the cultural strains of the 1960s, particularly student rebellions and opposition to American involvement in Vietnam. In ways that it had not previously, the American flag became an object of scorn and derision, yet also an object of hope enlisted in the cause of social change. It may seem inevitable that the flag would be burned and worn, waved and brandished, but for that to happen it had first to be demystified from a sacred emblem into something else, something more multivalent in meaning. That transformation first took root in cold-war America, and it was artists such as Jasper Johns and photographers such as Robert Frank who helped prepare the culture for the reexamination of America that was to come.

Born in 1930 and raised in the South, Jasper Johns, after service in the Korean War, settled in New York in 1953. In 1954–55, he painted *Flag*, and for years afterward Johns offered different versions of flags in different mediums. Johns also painted objects such as targets and numbers; his work marked a shift from abstract expressionism to the beginnings of pop art. He reclaimed everyday objects and compelled viewers to reimagine how they perceived "the things the mind already knows." His first flag image, Johns said,

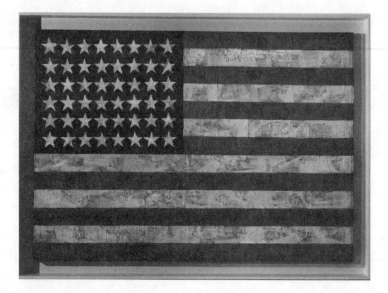

Jasper Johns, Flag, *1954–55. Encaustic, oil, and collage on fabric mounted on plywood, 42 1/4" × 60 5/8". Gift of Philip Johnson in honor of Alfred H. Barr, Jr. (106.1973).* (THE MUSEUM OF MODERN ART, NEW YORK, NY)

came to him in a dream. The work he produced, while seeming to be merely a straightforward painted reproduction of the flag, on closer view consists of layers and depths. Johns used a technique that allowed the paint to dry quickly yet also reveal the brushstrokes. The work also contains elements of collage that bleed through the surface. The result is a work that looks quite different when viewed from a distance than when seen up close, a work that could be read as celebrating the flag while also raising questions about its composition and meaning. In the paintings that followed, Johns would bleach the flag of its colors, producing monochromatic white and gray flags, paint multicolored flags with ghost images below, and superimpose flags upon one another so that they seem to be coming toward the viewer.

In the 1950s, Johns was not the only artist inviting viewers to rethink the meaning of the flag and their relationship to the object. In 1955, Robert Frank, a Swiss-born photographer who had emigrated to the United States in 1947, won a Guggenheim Fellowship for a proposal to travel the United States and photograph the America he encountered. His various road trips took him all over the country, and he shot thousands of pictures from which he chose a few dozen for his book *The Americans*, published first in France, then in the United States in 1959. The book, with its stunningly original photographic vision of the country, a vision in which the photographer seems willing to convey his feelings to the viewer, is a masterpiece of the ongoing attempt to come to terms with the meaning of America. Indeed, Jack Kerouac wrote the introduction to the book. Kerouac, whose seminal *On the Road* appeared in 1957, said that Frank had "sucked a sad, sweet poem out of America."

Frank's book opens with *Parade—Hoboken, New Jersey*. We are looking up at a building. Two figures in windows across from one another, separated by several feet of brick wall, are looking out. We can tell both are women, but the face of the figure on the left is in the shadow cast by a bright white shade. The head of the figure on the right cannot be seen at all. We only see her left hand going to her mouth. The bottom of a rippling American flag cuts off everything above. As one commentator notes, "The flag . . . is a kind of guillotine." Frank's photograph plays on light and texture. This would appear to be no celebratory depiction of American patriotism. The flag seems suspended in air, attached to no pole or visible

Robert Frank, Parade—Hoboken, New Jersey, *1955–56: copyright Robert Frank, from* The Americans (PACE/MACGILL GALLERY)

wire. The two spectators are trapped, dismembered witnesses to a parade.

Robert Frank's seemingly bleak assessment of America was part of a more general reevaluation of the meaning of the nation. In his poem "America" (1956), Allen Ginsberg declared:

America I've given you all and now I'm nothing.
America two dollars and twenty-seven cents January 17, 1956.
I can't stand my own mind.
America when will we end the human war?
Go fuck yourself with your atom bomb
I don't feel good don't bother me.
I won't write my poem till I'm in my right mind.

The meaning of America and the meaning of the flag went together. As the counterculture of the late 1950s and the 1960s came into prominence, attempts to redefine America often meant desacralizing the flag by wearing it. The cultural rebellions of the 1960s necessarily implicated the flag. Ginsberg came to sport a top hat with the American flag motif. In discussing Ken Kesey, the Merry Pranksters, and the drug culture of the 1960s, Ginsberg argued that "they didn't reject the American flag but instead washed it and took it back from the neoconservatives and right wingers and war hawks who were wrapping themselves in the flag, so Kesey painted the flag on his sneakers and had a little flag in his teeth filling." In 1969, the film *Easy Rider* featured Peter Fonda and Dennis Hopper on a road trip in search of themselves and the nation. In the film, Fonda is known as Captain America, and he sports an American flag helmet and motorcycle. Their search ends tragically as they encounter an America intolerant of difference.

If for some the flag became a symbol of what was wrong with America, an ironic symbol to be reappropriated in different ways, for others it was a symbol to be enlisted in the cause of making the nation a more just and democratic place. One of the striking, and shrewd, tactics of the civil rights movement for racial equality was for marchers and protesters to enlist the American flag in their struggle. Until the 1960s, the flag, given the history of racial oppression and segregation, was not a symbol that African Americans embraced. Henry McNeal Turner, bishop of the African Methodist Episcopal Church, spoke for many at the turn of the twentieth century when he declared, "to the Negro the American flag is a dirty and contemptible rag." When Kenneth Clark, the distinguished psychologist whose work played a key role in the decision of *Brown v. Board of Education*, focused his attention on

Harlem in the early 1960s, he encountered a man in his mid-thirties whom he quoted in his study *Dark Ghetto*: "The flag here in America is for the white man. The blue is for justice; the fifty white stars you see in the blue are for the fifty white states; and the white you see in it is the White House. It represents white folks. The red in it is the white man's blood—he doesn't even respect your blood, that's why he will lynch you, hang you, barbecue you, and fry you."

It is difficult to date with precision when civil rights activists realized that they needed to enlist the flag in their cause if ever they were going to feel represented by it. One key, early moment came in 1963 after Medgar Evers's assassination. Evers worked tirelessly in Mississippi in support of desegregation and voting rights. He led a boycott of white merchants in Jackson and, as field secretary for the NAACP, helped establish chapters across the state. He was gunned down outside his home on June 12, 1963. Two days later, on Flag Day, women and children marched through Jackson carrying small American flags. The idea had originated only weeks earlier with Evers himself. A World War II veteran, Evers watched time and again as the police smashed the signs of protesters. If they carried flags, perhaps the whole calculus of protest would shift.

On May 31, some six hundred students had marched down Capitol Street, "singing and waving American flags." The police took little mercy on them, grabbing the flags and beating the marchers. Two weeks later, Evers was dead. As protesters marched carrying small American flags, reporters could not believe what they witnessed—and photographed: the police used clubs against women and children with flags.

Thereafter, the flag became ubiquitous at civil rights marches, as images of the Selma to Montgomery March in 1965 make clear. After enduring a terrible beating when they first tried to march on behalf of voting rights, activists arrived in Montgomery and assembled in front of the Alabama state capitol. Charles Moore, a photographer for *Life*, documented the march. Moore, born in Alabama in 1931, had already distinguished himself for his exclusive photos from inside the administration building at the University of Mississippi, where James Meredith tried to enroll in 1962, and his searing photographs from Birmingham in 1963, when police used water hoses and dogs to attack protesters. At Montgomery, Moore found a spot facing the marchers, and he took a picture of the crowd. Hundreds of marchers, black and white, are pressed together. They carry and wave the American flag, dozens of which fill the air. They would hear Martin Luther King declare that "segregation is on its deathbed" and that "there never was a moment in American history more honorable and more inspiring than the pilgrimage of clergymen and laymen of every race and faith pouring into Selma to face danger at the side of its embattled Negroes."

Another photograph from the Selma to Montgomery March captured one man's embrace of the flag. James Karales was a staff photographer for *Look*. A 1955 graduate of Ohio University, he had served as an assistant to the distinguished magazine photographer W. Eugene Smith. In the image, the flag swirls around the shoulders of the marcher: it is his cape, his crown, or, potentially, his winding sheet. The youth's face is serious, focused. The sunshine hits his eyes, a white stripe across his face, but he stares intently ahead. The stripes of his shirt mirror the stripes of the flag. His hand rests beneath the fabric, holding it aloft on a simple wooden pole. The flag is his comfort and his hope. He, along with other civil rights activists,

Charles Moore, Alabama, *1965* (BLACK STAR)

had appropriated Old Glory to the cause and enlisted it on the side of justice.

If the fight for equality led African Americans to embrace the flag, opposition by intransigent southerners could lead civil rights proponents to burn it. On the afternoon of June 6, 1966, in Brooklyn, New York, Sydney Street, a middle-aged bus driver and a World War II veteran, heard on the radio that James Meredith had been shot in Mississippi, a day after embarking on a "march against fear" to encourage blacks to vote. Street took from his drawer his folded forty-eight-star American flag and carried it to a major intersection near his home. He set the flag on fire and dropped it to the pavement, where it lay burning. A few dozen people gathered, and an approaching police officer heard Street

James Karales, Selma to Montgomery Civil Rights March, *1965* (ESTATE OF JAMES KARALES)

say, "If they let that happen to Meredith, we don't need an American flag."

Meredith would recover from his wounds and rejoin the march at the end of June. Meanwhile, on Flag Day, in Granada, Mississippi, marchers placed an American flag on a Confederate monument. In New York, Street was charged with a misdemeanor and given a suspended sentence. His appeal found its way to the Supreme Court, where a split Court reversed the conviction on the grounds that it wasn't clear whether Street was convicted solely for burning the flag or for his speech as well. The decision did not protect flag burning as a form of speech; it only reaffirmed that words used against the flag were constitutionally protected.

By the time the Court decided *Street* in 1969, flag burning had become something of an epidemic. Across the country, protesters against the Vietnam War expressed their opposition by burning the American flag. These incidents reached a peak in 1967 when, at an anti-war rally in New York's Central Park, a protester burned the flag and cameras recorded the event. Paul Krassner, founder of the *Realist*, a satirical countercultural magazine published from 1958 to 1974, and one of the cofounders of the Yippies, recalled that "in April 1967, at an anti-war rally in Central Park, I observed a hippie wandering around with a loaf of whole grain bread, looking for others to share it with, when he was approached by somebody with an American flag in one hand and a can of lighter fluid in the other. 'Would you hold this?' he asked. The hippie held the flag while the stranger set it on fire." Within weeks the House Judiciary Committee convened hearings, and Congress debated passage of a bill that made it a criminal offense to "cast contempt upon any flag of the United States."

Photographs of the Central Park flag burning especially roiled members of Congress, who repeatedly made reference to the images during the debate. Basil Whitener of North Carolina averred that "of all the photographs which I have seen in my lifetime, I have never been as immediately and as heavily repulsed." Richard Poff of Virginia said the photographs "pictured the flag in a posture of obscenity." Jerry Pettis of California reminded the chamber that "nothing has sickened the American people so thoroughly as accounts and pictures of unwashed, irreverent gangs burning and otherwise desecrating Old Glory." And Dan Kuykendall of Tennessee asked rhetorically, "Which is the greater contribution to the security of freedom: the inspiring photo of the marines raising the flag on a bloody hill at Iwo Jima, or the shameful pictures of unshaven beatniks burning that same flag in Central Park in New York?"

Not everyone embraced the bill. Congressmen such as John Conyers of Michigan and Don Edwards of California raised questions about its constitutionality and advisability. "This legislation," they argued, "would infringe upon what is certainly one of the most basic of freedoms, the freedom of dissent." Conyers and Edwards were two of only sixteen who voted against the bill, which passed in the House with 387 voting yes (thirty did not vote). It sailed through the Senate as well, and in 1968 the first Federal Flag Desecration law went into effect. Any person found guilty of "publicly mutilating, defacing, defiling, burning or trampling" the flag faced a thousand-dollar fine and/or up to a year in prison.

At the very moment that the burning of the flag as a protest against the Vietnam War gained national attention, the flag also began to appear as an object used and depicted by artists as an object of scorn. In 1967, a New York art gallery owner, Stephen Radich, exhibited sixteen anti-war paintings and sculptures by Marc Morrell. The window display on the second floor showed a flag stuffed to resemble a cadaver and hanging from chains. Among the works inside the gallery was an erect phallus covered with a flag. Radich was arrested and convicted of violating a New York flag-desecration law.

Artists continued to employ the flag in their work to protest not only the war but also civil injustice. In 1967, Faith Ringgold painted *The Flag Is Bleeding*. The 72"×96" canvas depicts a black man, a white woman, and a white man, standing with arms interlocked beneath the red and white stripes. The black man has been stabbed in the heart (or has stabbed himself; he holds what appears to be a knife in his left hand), and his blood drips upon the flag. In 1971, Wayne Eagleboy painted *We the People,* a work that depicts two Indians behind barbed wire that serves as the stars of the flag; the painting is framed in fur. In response to the arrest and conviction of Radich, artists in 1970 contributed to a People's Flag Show at the Judson Memorial Church in Greenwich Village. The text for a poster for the show read: "The American people are the only people who can interpret the American Flag. A flag which does not belong to the people to do with as they see fit should be burned and forgotten. Artists, workers, students, women, third world peoples—you are oppressed—what does the flag mean to you? Join the people's answer to the repressive US government and state laws restricting our use and display of the flag."

Authorities shut down the show after the opening night, but among the works displayed was Kate Millett's sculpture *The American Dream Goes to Pot.* The piece shows an American flag stuffed into a toilet housed inside a wooden cage. Millett, best known for her feminist work, recalls: "We were expressing our solidarity with our fellow artist and our right to use the flag as a sort of symbolic language of our dislike of the policy of the war in Vietnam." By then, even Jasper Johns had created a flag image that was explicitly political. For Moratorium Day in 1969, a day for mass demonstrations against the Vietnam War, Johns contributed a silk screen that became the poster for the event. It depicts a sickly flag, not in red, white, and blue, but in green, black, and orange, a flag that perhaps evokes the jungles of Vietnam. At the center of the flag is a single white dot—a bullet hole.

In the late 1960s, Americans were burning and redesigning the flag, and they were wearing it as well. In April 1968, *Hair* opened on Broadway, and during one musical number the flag is used to clothe

Faith Ringgold, The American People Series, #18, The Flag Is Bleeding, *1967* (COURTESY FAITH RINGGOLD)

a naked body. When the show came to Boston two years later, the head of the entertainment licensing bureau opined that anyone "who abuses the American flag should be horsewhipped in public on Boston Common." In October 1968, Abbie Hoffman, one of the leaders of the Yippies, wore an American flag shirt to protest a hearing by the House Un-American Activities Committee. He was arrested and harrassed. At his trial he said, "I wore the shirt to show that we were in the tradition of the founding fathers of this country," and when found guilty he declared, "I only regret that I have but one shirt to give for my country."

Dismayed and disgruntled by what they saw as the abuse of the flag, a very different group of Americans, construction workers, rioted on May 8, 1970. Wearing flag decals on their hard hats, and waving Old Glory in the air, they marched to Wall Street to break up a student anti-war demonstration. The construction workers started beating the protesters. According to one youth, "We came here to express our sympathy for those killed at Kent State and they attacked us with lead pipes wrapped in American flags." From Wall Street, where they placed American flags on the statue of George Washington, the hard hats marched to City Hall, where they successfully demanded that the flag, flying at half mast to honor the four students killed in Ohio four days earlier, be raised. Those who protested the war and those who defended it, those who thought the flag was being defiled by the policies of the United States government and those who thought that to defile the flag was to be a traitor, now came adorned in red, white, and blue.

The question of the constitutionality of wearing the flag reached the Supreme Court from a case that originated in Massachusetts. In January 1970, two police officers in Leominster spotted a young man named Goguen with a 4"×6" cloth version of the American flag sewn to his pants. When officers approached the youth, Goguen's friends laughed. A complaint was sworn out against him for violating the contempt provision of the Massachusetts flag statute that begins "Whoever publicly mutilates, tramples upon, defaces or treats contemptuously the flag of the United States." A jury found Goguen guilty, and the Massachusetts Supreme Judicial Court affirmed the decision. The district court overturned the conviction, finding the language of the contempt portion of the statute unconstitutional. The Court of Appeals and the Supreme Court, in a 6–3 decision in *Smith v. Goguen* (1974), agreed. Justice Lewis Powell argued that "in a time of widely varying attitudes and tastes for displaying something as ubiquitous as the United States flag or representations of it, it could hardly be the purpose of the Massachusetts Legislature to make criminal every informal use of the flag. The statutory language under which Goguen was charged, however, fails to draw reasonably clear lines between the kinds of nonceremonial treatment that are criminal and those that are not. Due process requires that 'all be informed as to what the State commands or forbids' . . . Given today's tendencies to treat the flag unceremoniously, these notice standards are not satisfied here."

Three months after *Smith v. Goguen*, the Supreme Court would decide one more major flag case. In *Spence v. Washington*, the appellant, a college student, was appealing his conviction under an "improper use" statute for flying an American flag, with the peace symbol taped to it, upside down from his apartment. The Court, in a 6–3 decision, overturned the conviction as a clear "case of prosecution for the expression of an idea through activity." Spence had every right to use his private property in a peaceful way to express his beliefs, in this case protesting the killings at Kent State and American involvement overseas. The activity was a form of communication protected by the First Amendment. In his dissent, Justice William Rehnquist thought the state had the power to withdraw "a unique national symbol from the roster of materials that may be used as a background for communications."

The tension between communication and desecration polarized the Court, and most Americans, on different sides of the debate. On July 6, 1970, *Time* magazine placed the "Fight over the Flag" on its cover and observed that "what was once an easy, automatic rite of patriotism has become in many cases a considered political act, burdened with overtones and conflicting meanings greater than Old Glory was ever meant to bear. In the tug of war for the nation's will and soul, the flag has somehow become the symbolic rope."

Through the 1960s and into the 1970s, the flag had been displayed, waved, erected, decaled, flushed, torn, and burned. And then came Forman's photograph of Rakes using the flag as a weapon to assault a black man. For all the trampling, defacing, defiling, and mutilating that had been witnessed, this act seemed unimaginable, an act of desecration that slashed the fabric of the nation. One letter printed in the *Globe* no doubt spoke for many. Referring to the photograph, the writer "felt horror and repugnance at the desecration of our symbol of freedom and liberty." Several days after the assault, David Wilson, a *Globe* columnist, began by referring to the conviction of Goguen, which drew the applause of "professional patriots." "One cannot help wondering," he continued, "whether those same professional patriots regard as desecration and subversion the use of the flagstaff streaming Old Glory to bash the face of a lawyer set upon by a mob while pursuing his lawful calling outside City Hall." Wilson denounced all "those patriotic societies and organizations presumably devoted to preventing the misuse" of the flag for their "thunderous silence." He implored these very groups, who he thought were probably conservative on the question of busing, to "be the first to express outrage." Wilson took a global view of the incident and wondered about its impact abroad: "It is difficult to imagine a dramatic scenario with more poisonous consequences for American influence and, yes, national security, than the repulsive and nauseating spectacle of white hoodlums ganging up on a black man, and beating on him with the national emblem of the 'land of the free and home of the brave.' In distant places, Americans labor mightily

Robert Mapplethorpe, American Flag, *1977* (THE ROBERT MAPPLETHORPE FOUNDATION)

against formidable adversaries and great odds to try to explain to citizens of other countries that America is not an oppressive, racist, and evil place."

Within weeks of the incident at City Hall Plaza, most Bostonians and most other Americans would turn their attention to celebrating the Bicentennial of a nation they viewed as a free, democratic, and beneficent place. The image of the flag appeared everywhere: on cups, plates, mugs, clocks, cufflinks, magnets, ashtrays, snow-domes, pens, pillowcases, T-shirts, bikinis, even toilet paper. "I see no harm in these Bicentennial products," said a member of the Sons of the

American Revolution. "There is no harm in making a buck." Others took a less sanguine view. One historian labeled the entire enterprise "Bicentennial Schlock," a crass, commercial extravaganza that further sullied the meaning of the American Revolution.

The following year, Robert Mapplethorpe, who was at the beginning of his photographic career, took a picture of the American flag that serves as a coda to the era. In the Polaroid image, a tattered flag on a vertical pole waves across a soupy sky. The sun burns from behind the flag's stars, a bulb of light ready to ignite the fabric. Threadbare and torn, the flag sways, but its days are numbered and it hangs beyond repair.

CHAPTER 5

THE IMPACT

AMERICANS AWOKE ON April 6 to the image of a white youth assaulting a black man with the flag. *The Soiling of Old Glory* appeared on front pages across the country. The *Washington Post* placed it at top center, above the fold; in the *Chicago Tribune*, it was featured below the headline about Howard Hughes's death; the *San Francisco Chronicle* carried it top center, with the caption "Racial Beating in Boston"; editors placed it at the top right of the *Hartford Courant*. The *New York Times* printed the photograph inside the paper with the caption "Violence in Boston." The incident was also reported on the ABC national television news with Harry Reasoner. As Reasoner narrated the story of Landsmark's beating, the camera panned across the photograph. Later in the year, the Socialist Workers Party used the image as a presidential election poster: "200 Years of Racism Is Enough!" (The candidate received the most votes in the history of the party.) The photograph also appeared around the world, including newspapers in England, Germany, and Egypt. But the national and international papers and media did not grasp what the citizens of Boston understood: the photograph revealed more than an incident of racial violence. It showed a city, in the year of the Bicentennial, at war with itself and a heritage it had once been proud to bestow on the nation.

In the immediate aftermath of the assault on Ted Landsmark, the mayor called on the police commissioner to investigate and issue arrest warrants. "It was racism pure and simple," declared Mayor White, "not a fight over busing." He added that "from the vantage point of a City Hall office it was clear that this attack, like so many, was the work of only a few thugs." Mayor White also sought to defend himself against the accusations that he stood above the fray watching and did not act: "I sprang for the door and tried to get down there but the whole thing had broken up by then."

Whatever the mayor's actions at the time of the assault, he made certain that arrests came quickly. The first arrest came the day after the assault, April 6, when a South Boston youth, age sixteen, was charged with delinquency and two counts of assault and battery and released on personal recognizance. On April 8, Edward Irvin, seventeen, the junior class president at Charlestown High School, was charged with assault and battery.

Municipal Court Judge Harry Elam called the attack "one of the most vicious incidents ever to take place in this city. I was born in this city and have lived here all my life. But I have never seen anything so disgraceful to the city as this attack on a respected citizen." Two of the men accompanying Irvin were wearing buttons that read STOP FORCED BUSING. A third student, a fifteen-year-old from Madison Park High School, appeared with his parents after learning of a warrant issued in his name. Finally, on April 12, a week after the attack, police made a fourth arrest. Joseph Rakes, age seventeen, was identified as a student at the Heights Academy. It was he who wielded the flag.

Governor Dukakis issued a statement: "I am appalled by the senseless and unprovoked attack on Ted Landsmark at City Hall

Plaza. A man who has worked tirelessly to build a better city for black and white alike was victimized solely because of the color of his skin . . . Mob violence of this sort cannot be tolerated. The youths who did the beating only harm their own cause through such savagery. I hope all persons who were involved will be apprehended and prosecuted to the full extent of the law."

The day after the assault, on the morning of Tuesday, April 6, Ione Malloy, a teacher at South Boston High School, told her students "how disappointed I was about the attack on Landsmark, that they only hurt themselves by such incidents." The students were subdued and looked to an empty seat in the class that belonged, they knew, to the classmate who was at that moment being arrested. What shocked Malloy was that he was "a member of the integrated basketball team . . . [and] had never shown the slightest racial anger." When he returned to class, she scolded him and gave him a small part in the play they were reading. That afternoon, the teachers met at a crisis prevention seminar and "agreed that the student body was depressed and ashamed about the incident." At the same time, most students seemed to have become indifferent to the consequences of their actions. One senior told Malloy, "Look at Landsmark. Those kids knew the police were there, but they didn't care." They were prepared to be arrested.

As the South Boston High School students returned to class, legislators gathered at the statehouse to begin their business. The calendar called for a fairly typical day. There were bills to be passed for debate, reports on bills, and bills referred back to committee. But before any of the Orders of the Day were to be considered, the members debated a resolution offered by the Republican whip, William Robinson of Melrose.

Regardless of where they stood on the issue of busing, legislators were outraged and dismayed by the events and images from City Hall Plaza. Robinson's resolution cast the blame widely:

Whereas, There took place on City Hall Plaza yesterday, an unprovoked assault on a twenty-nine-year-old black man by certain people who claimed they were present to peacefully demonstrate against court ordered busing; and

["A"] Whereas, Another 250 onlookers found it morally possible to stand by and watch the beating without trying to stop it; and

["B"] Whereas, Newspaper and television reporters in the crowd somehow found it morally possible to spend their time taking pictures of the beating, rather than trying to stop it; and

["C"] Whereas, The Mayor of Boston found it morally possible to view the beating from a window in City Hall, and do nothing to try and stop it; and

["D"] Whereas, The Boston Police found it morally possible to spend their time practicing effective crowd control while a man was being whipped with a flag pole, without trying to stop it; and

["E"] Whereas, The conduct yesterday of all parties, save the victim, was spineless, and immoral: therefore, be it

Resolved. The Massachusetts House of Representatives by passing these resolutions declares its sense of outrage at this senseless beating and expresses its growing impatience with the existing chaos and violent temper of the City of Boston.

Not knowing whom to blame, in frustration and anger Robinson's resolutions indicted everyone but Landsmark. Robinson was also fearful of the black community's response. According to the minutes of the House of Representatives, he defended his resolution by arguing that "we as a mostly white Legislature should express our outrage, so the black community will know how we feel. The black community will even the score and there is no telling what they will do. It's incredible to see smiling faces of the crowd on the paper's front page and the beating on TV cameras."

Francis Doris of Revere spoke for many exhausted over the busing crisis: "These occurrences cannot be allowed to happen. When I see our flag rammed into a man's face, I get sick and every one of us should, during this Bicentennial more than ever, we should say our symbol of American heritage should not be used as a weapon of hatred. It was a dastardly act, and our children should hear that."

Melvin King, an African American representative from Boston, argued that the resolutions "should not be framed in black and white terms, but in terms of what's right and what's wrong. There's no question in my mind that the seeds of fascist behavior were exemplified by what happened in Boston yesterday . . . If we refuse to accept the responsibility for this, if we sit silently by, then we are saying we support what happened. Those people inciting youngsters to be fascist are not just anti-black, they're anti-human."

King asked for a roll call on the vote, and it was granted. The majority whip, George Keverian of Everett, then moved an amendment to the resolutions. He moved to strike the four paragraphs of "Whereas" that indicted the spectators, the press, the mayor, and the police for standing by and watching the beating without trying to stop it. Keverian denounced the charges as unfair. Not all the onlookers were smiling, he said. The newsmen weren't laughing. The mayor was not individually responsible for what took place several stories below his office window.

Robinson responded by declaring that he was mad at the world: "The police were more interested in crowd control. Shame on the mayor, he could have gone downstairs. The press was taking pictures. That man was more important than that news story. What would have happened had it been a white man? Those thugs have caused Dame Boston to hang her head in shame, and I say we ought to say something about it."

For the next hour the House debate turned angry, and accusations of racism, so much a part of everyday discourse outside the chamber, now flowed inside. Michael Flaherty of South Boston denounced Robinson's posturing as "theatrics" and proclaimed that "the South Boston community and Charlestown community were 100 percent against what took place yesterday." He then asked where Robinson's outrage was when whites were attacked by blacks—a sixty-eight-year-old fisherman who had been stoned, for example. "We have lived through this," he declared. "We know what's wrong with the city. We don't know what went on behind the scenes. I'd just like to say to the world we in Boston were against this and apologize for it."

African American freshman representative Robert Fortes of Boston thought the disease of racism was everywhere, including the body of which he was a member. "I wonder why I came here at all," he averred, "because I realize how racist this hall is. We pass something but we don't deal with human issues . . . I've heard our colleagues make racist remarks. You say you represent the people, but in many cases you represent individuals who are sick and can't deal with what's happening. I'm sick of looking at my children and telling them the system works, because now I don't know. For once, look into your hearts and ask what's wrong. If you want a bloodbath in

Boston or the state, keep on. I've been ashamed as a freshman in this house . . . You're supporting what happened by merely saying we'll condemn it but won't press the issue of whether the mayor was standing in the window."

Others opposed Keverian's amendment. The mayor should be condemned as irresponsible; the onlookers should be condemned as spineless; the press should be condemned as biased. Francis Coppinger of Boston asked if anyone knew of the "two white boys who had gasoline poured on them[.] One died, and we know the color of their assailants, but we probably never heard of the case." Referring to Landsmark he said, "I saw the fellow on the news last night, and saw no marks on his face, but he was shown in the morning paper with bandages on his face. I hope we take no action until we have a complete study of what's going on in Boston schools, because yesterday was the result of all that we've been afraid to expose."

With the chamber reaching a boiling point, a few representatives called for calm and offered hope that cooler thoughts would prevail. One read a quotation from the Bible about people who still have life though they appear to be dead. By voice vote, the amendment was adopted. By a roll call vote of 216–0, the resolution condemning the assault passed. Two representatives, including Coppinger, voted present. Twenty others did not answer the roll call.

Later in the day, members of the Black Legislative Caucus and other black community leaders gathered at City Hall Plaza, yards away from the scene of the previous day's assault. A crowd of two hundred heard State Senator William Owens of Mattapan issue a series of demands that called for the attorney general to investigate the role of the City Council and the School Committee in "inciting young people to mob violence," asked that federal funds be withheld from the city until access to all was guaranteed, and withdrew his vote of confidence in Mayor Kevin White.

Still more provocative were the comments of the Rev. Rafe Taylor, pastor of the Ebenezer Baptist Church and member of the Black Ecumenical Council: "War is being declared against black folks in Boston . . . The question we must now ask is—is it time we armed ourselves and started to protect our own rights?" Black leaders declared that "people of color are not safe to come here to Boston and we are asking people of color across the nation to stay away. We issue a call for all persons of color to band together because it is now that this bizarre situation of outright racism in Boston must stop. We must come to the realization that if Boston state officials will not protect us, we must ask for Federal protection."

Elsewhere in the city, Vernon Jordan, executive director of the National Urban League, denounced the attack and raised questions about Boston, which was scheduled to host the Urban League's annual convention in August. "I am not sure I'm glad to be in Boston because I am not sure I am safe and will be protected here," Jordan confessed. The silence of the white community seemed deafening to him, and he insisted that every institution in Boston was on trial before the world. Using a phrase made infamous by Malcolm X after President Kennedy's assassination, he declared: "The chickens have come home to roost. This great state of the abolitionists must get its house in order because if you are not careful that same region you told ten years ago to straighten up and fly right will show you the way to a peaceful, open, pluralistic society." Jordan concluded by noting that if such an attack could occur at City Hall, it could occur anywhere, and if blacks were not safe, then neither were whites. "We must live together as people," he said, "or die together as fools."

Two weeks later, black novelist James Baldwin, visiting Cambridge to promote a new book, commented on the assault. He viewed busing as a distraction from the real issues of power and class that always were at work in American society. Baldwin said that "the kids were raised to do what they are doing. There is a whole social and economic structure in this town—in this country—that's responsible for their lawlessness." The real problem, he insisted, was neither busing nor desegregated schools but property and real estate interests. Poor blacks and poor whites fight each other because that is "an American tradition" through which the wealthy maintain power. "It's ironic," concluded Baldwin, "that in this city, where they held the goddamed tea party 200 years ago, black people are forced to say the same thing 200 years later—no taxation without representation."

Political leaders opposed to busing had their own reactions. None, of course, defended the assault on Landsmark, but they instead sought to reframe the issue away from racism and back toward the problem of busing as a means of achieving desegregation and toward the apparent bias of the media.

Louise Day Hicks, who had invited the protesters to City Hall, issued no public statement and observed only that if Mayor White resigned, as some black officials demanded, she would become mayor in her capacity as City Council president. She declared it an ironic vote of confidence in her by the black caucus and chuckled that if she became mayor "there would be an end to all the city's problems."

James Kelly also held a press conference. The president of the South Boston Information Center, Kelly had accompanied the students to City Hall. Kelly denounced the assault as "unfortunate and ugly" and emphasized that "violent incidents cannot be condoned." He also offered legal and moral support to the arrested students. He feared that the coverage of the incident distracted from the "legiti-mate demands of the students." Rakes was a "legitimately good kid," Kelly said. He added that "if it wasn't for the tension in the city of Boston, an incident like that could never have happened. It all stems from forced busing." Kelly blistered Judge Garrity, who, by his un-constitutional decree to forcibly integrate the city of Boston, had brought the city to its knees financially. And now, even worse, Bos-tonians were "bordering dangerously close to what only can be re-garded as a potential race war."

The anti-busing leader went on to denounce the media. "More than half of the root of the problem is the liberal media," he insisted, and he wondered why there were so few news reports of assaults by blacks, including one on a white bus driver in Roxbury. Kelly talked about fear, the fear whites and blacks held for one another. He said that whites stayed away from Roxbury and Dorchester because "fear of these areas for ourselves and for our children is a very real fear. This fear is the predominant factor in refusing to be any part of Judge Garrity's social engineering plan. Blacks are not unacceptable to us, but black crime is."

TWO DAYS AFTER the assault, on April 7, Theodore Landsmark held a press conference at the Harriet Tubman House, in a room crowded with supporters and the press. He arrived in a gray three-piece suit, with a huge bandage covering his nose. Tape ran up toward his fore-head and across his cheeks. The excessive bandaging was inten-tional. At the hospital, a black doctor treated him and said he could have a small bandage that would suffice to cover the broken nose or something more dramatic. Wanting to make an impact, wanting to

Ted Landsmark bandaged, 1976 (BOSTON HERALD AMERICAN)

remind reporters of the viciousness of the assault, he emerged with tape covering much of his face. Because of his nose, Landmark's voice sounded nasal, and he apologized for it. His left eye was puffy and bloodshot.

He began by trying to resolve some tensions in the room between union and nonunion press. He said he had done union organizing but that the issue was too large to be fought over at the press conference. He asked for cooperation and proceeded with his prepared remarks, which he delivered with an even, forceful tone.

He said he wasn't prepared for the kind of national and

international publicity that he had received as a result of the incident, and that he was trying to rest because he had lost a fair amount of blood, but that he thought it important to offer a statement:

> I am making myself available to the media today, despite the extent of my injuries, and my need to rest, because I am deeply concerned that the drama of my being beaten in front of City Hall and the response that that incident has elicited may overshadow and distort certain issues which are critical, in my judgment, to Boston's future and to the well-being of blacks and whites who work in Boston. These are issues to which I have devoted my life and my work and I am now as much injured by their distortion as from the physical assault which I incurred this past Monday.
>
> First I wish to make a few comments about the attack itself. For the most part, the sequence of events has been recorded accurately. I was on my way to an affirmative action liaison committee meeting with the Boston Redevelopment Authority to discuss certain construction contracts which are about to be let to the South End of Boston. I was taken by surprise and I was beaten and kicked by a crowd of young people coming from an anti-busing rally at City Hall. It is not correct that Deputy Mayor Jones was on the scene with me and ran away. I greatly regret that Mr. Jones' actions have been misreported by certain of the wire services. I particularly regret any suggestions that he ran away because Jeep [a nickname for Clarence Jones] was the first person, and to my knowledge the only person, who left City Hall to come to my aid. Jeep escorted me to an ambulance, spent the entire morning with me at the hospital, and only left when at my suggestion I felt his services were no longer needed. His leaving

City Hall when he did was in my judgment an extremely courageous action. From the films which I reviewed this morning, he appears to be about the only person who did leave City Hall to come out to my assistance as I staggered around City Hall Plaza.

Secondly, I wish to make clear that I intend at this time to seek all legal courses of action to secure remedies that are available to me. I have consulted with attorneys and I intend to see that all those responsible for the violence of this nature are fully prosecuted. I intend to take such legal actions as are necessary, pursuing both criminal and civil remedies against certain members of the Boston City Council and the Boston School Committee to ensure that the Boston City Hall can no longer be used as a sanctuary for racism and as a resource center for those who would incite and encourage racist violence and for those who would perpetuate the less dramatic but more effective day to day pattern of discrimination against people of color in Boston.

Third, I want to express my appreciation for the many acts of kindness and courage which have been directed towards me as a result of my having been an object of this attack. It is encouraging to see a positive and constructive response from many persons in the black and white communities who have been silent for too long. I would point out that such commitment, particularly from the white community, could have prevented much of the racial hostility in Boston had they been made meaningful prior to the violence. I appreciate the strong and immediate response of the Black Caucus. I appreciate the strong support given to me by the board of directors of the Contractors Association of Boston, my employers, and by the Massachusetts Black Lawyers Association. I have been very deeply touched by the kindness and what seems to be a very genuine concern of individuals who have called me, some as far away as San Francisco, from all over the country. I also want to express my thanks to the news photographers and TV cameramen at the scene who held their ground and kept their cameras steady in the face of a lot of confusion and danger. I should note as a sidelight that I have done some photojournalism myself and I know that what you folks did was very difficult. Of course I wish that someone, as a simple act of humanity, had come to help me. But I do not know if that was really possible. I do note that without the photographic record that those of you in the media established it would be highly improbable that a remedy would be available to me and the incident would have ended up being recorded as just another scuffle on the streets of City Hall Plaza.

I've worked for a number of years on economic and social development issues in communities of color and other econom- ically depressed areas throughout the east coast. Racism is the apparent direct cause of Monday's unprovoked attack on me. But such racism has been fueled, by my judgment, by selfish political leaders who have been unable or unwilling to address themselves much more seriously to the hardcore economic and social problems Boston faces. We continue to need jobs and housing and high quality education and human decency for all the people of Boston and I will continue to work toward those ends. Retaliatory violence will not solve these problems, but continued work by those of us in communities of color to strengthen our communities will. We have now the economic and political strength to come to solutions for these problems. And Monday's attack, to my mind, only underlines the necessity of our using our economic and political strength for the better social benefit for all of us. I think it unfortunate that the attack on me is already being used by some people for their own narrow ends and justifications. The issue goes far beyond safety in the streets. We can not solve complex problems with simplistic solutions or with emotional overreactions.

My first thoughts when I got to my feet in City Hall Plaza and I saw Chief Jones was to get to the Mayor to discuss matters of affirmative action in city contracting which seriously need his attention. You will note as you review those films that I stood up and kept on my way in toward City Hall because it was clear to me it's what my purpose for being at City Hall was on Monday. While I do not agree with the statement that Diane DeSantis of the Department of Justice has made that this is an isolated incident, I do feel that the issue of safety is only a small part of the problem. We must avoid being exploited and having this act of violence exploited to distract attention from the complex and extremely urgent problem of the life of this city and the lives of black and white people and all colored people in this city. Safety is not the issue. Busing is not the issue. The issue involves the participation of citizens of color in all levels of business and government that affects the life of this city, and by that I mean participation on an equal basis and not just as human rights officers and affirmative action officers and not just as shields to cover the white power structure's indifference toward communities of color. The issue of racism must no longer be subordinated in this city. Federal, state, local officials must act now to enforce all of the law. By that I mean not just the law with respect to safety but all the body of civil rights and affirmative action law which affects programs in this city. Business, both of color and white, and government must start to work now purposively to create a sound economic environment within the communities in which citizens of color now live and work and that includes City Hall Plaza.

The liaison committee that I was on my way to participate in at City Hall is one example of contractors and community citizens and government officials of color and white working together effectively to increase minority participation in city construction projects, to resolve mutual problems and to provide ultimate benefits to all the people of Boston.

My legal actions now are inevitably tied to the purpose of my presence in City Hall Plaza last Monday. While I have been hurt and wronged personally by the attack, it is people of color and humanity everywhere who will benefit from a satisfactory resolution of Boston's problems.

It was a remarkable public statement, delivered in a measured tone. Landsmark showed political savvy well beyond his twenty-nine years. He expressed thanks for all the support he had received; he cleared the deputy mayor, who was misidentified as the other black man present when the assault began; he acknowledged the critical role of the media, even while taking a swipe at the photographers for not lending a hand. Landsmark announced his intention to sue, but the lawyer never filed papers. What he wanted was to get the city's attention, and to redefine the problem into something much broader than even busing and desegregation: the problem of economic inequality and social injustice. Amid the turmoil and the outrage, Landsmark was thinking clearly. He had his eye on building communities of mutuality across race and class lines, communities that, if brought to fruition, would transform the city of Boston. After the assault, Landsmark had called his mother in New York, and she said, "Well, we've always known Boston is the kind of racist town where it is nicer to visit than to live." He answered, "I think blacks have to fight it out here." It might take time, but Landsmark wasn't going anywhere.

LETTERS AND COLUMNS in newspapers all tried to come to terms with the assault. Dave O'Brian, writing in the *Boston Phoenix*, a weekly alternative paper that covered news and arts, summarized the disbelief of many by pointing to the "overabundance of irony: black man beaten with American flag while walking across a public plaza (within screaming distance, one might add, of such Bicentennial attractions as Faneuil Hall and the Boston Massacre site) while on his way to an affirmative action meeting."

On April 10, the *Boston Herald American* titled its mailbag "The Beating of Theodore Landsmark." For a number of writers, Forman's photograph evoked religious thoughts of crucifixion and martyrdom. One writer thought that Forman's front page photograph "brings to mind the Stations of the Cross." Another writer observed: "They stand at attention, their hands on their hearts, pledging allegiance to the flag. Immediately afterwards, the steel shaft of that same flag is used to bludgeon a defenseless man to the ground where he is kicked and beaten. On the sidelines, their cohorts grin and cheer . . . It has always been said that our hope for the future lies with our young people. If this is a sample of what we may expect then may the good Lord deliver us." Another writer called Landsmark "just one in a long line of innocent people who have shed their blood. Why? Because he is black and he happened to be in a place where hatred was festering. We remember another mob scene where people were inhumane to an innocent man—Calvary."

Others commented on the hypocrisy of patriotism and violence: students pledging allegiance to the flag in the morning and then attacking with the same flag in the afternoon. "Shades of Adolf Hitler," thought one writer. The photographs and reports "filled my eyes with tears, my soul with despair, and my mind with horror . . . Almost as dreadful and terrifying as the crime itself are the faces of the onlookers. Some are actually smiling." Forman's front page photograph, wrote another contributor, shows "how low America has fallen. It shows who really runs this country, what caliber of intelligence runs this country . . . Yeah, let freedom ring, in the hands of a demented white man and his flag of freedom." "I thought the picture of the boy running the American flag into Landsmark was disgusting," said another letter, which concluded, "If that wasn't anti-American, nothing is." One woman asked, "Doesn't it remind you somehow of that oldie of the Marines raising the flag on Iwo Jima? What a picture. Let's have a few thousand giant posters made of it and nailed up all over the city. The perfect motif for Beautiful Boston's Bicentennial."

Some writers expressed concern about a media double standard. One letter from East Boston focused on racism but wondered about the racism of black attacks on whites. Where was the outcry against racism, he wondered, "when a group of black children stoned and stabbed a white man to death when he was fishing at Columbia Point two years ago? . . . Nothing grows from nothing. To grow flowers, fruit or vegetables we plant seeds and water them. The seeds of racism and violence were planted by Judge Garrity and watered by Mayor White, and now the city of Boston must reap the harvest." Another letter raised the question of racial attitudes in a different way. Why, he wondered, did the headline in the *Herald* read "Youths Beat Black Lawyer at City Hall"? Shouldn't it have read "White Youths Beat Black Lawyer" or "Youths Beat Lawyer at City Hall"?

The *Boston Globe* ran letters on the incident on two separate occasions. For a decade, opponents of busing had objected to the *Globe*'s coverage of desegregation and busing, accusing the editorial staff, most of whom, they pointed out, lived in the suburbs and were Protestants, of promoting a liberal agenda at all costs. Members of ROAR denounced the paper, boycotted it, and at times even lay down in front of trucks delivering it. "The *Globe*," one protester recalled, "was the enemy." That Forman's photograph appeared in the rival *Herald* did not seem to matter. It was the *Globe* that was unfair to the residents of South Boston and Charlestown.

The initial batch of letters, published on April 9, included some denouncing the *Globe*'s coverage as racist. One writer, echoing a *Herald* reader's letter, complained about the headline "Black Man Beaten by Young Busing Protesters," and argued that "if race is so integral to a story that one participant must be so identified, then all participants must be identified in a like manner." Another went farther and offered support for "the courageous people of South Boston who are constantly maligned by your newspaper." Accusing the *Globe* of holding a double standard, she wrote that "if your newspaper cited the rapes, muggings, arson, and murders performed by the 'blacks' you would have enough sensationalist material for years."

Other letters denounced the "defamation and complete

prostitution of the flag" and called for all to "join the struggle . . . to redeem the American flag from those who would use it as a weapon of racial intimidation." The assault was "not only an attack on the civil rights of one man but also on the foundations of American democracy."

It is unclear why, ten days later, the *Globe* devoted its morning and evening editions to a sampling of additional letters received by the editors. Perhaps, given its reputation as a newspaper that supported busing, the editors wanted readers to know that the public response was overwhelmingly against the anti-busing protesters. In an italicized headnote, the editors said they had received eighty-nine letters, eighty-six of which "denounced or deplored the incident." Most of the letters expressed outrage, shame, disgust, repugnance, and sorrow. Several directly attacked the opponents of busing and the parents of the protesters: "Louise Day Hicks tells us she is not against black people—only busing. On April 5, she invited a group of youths into the City Council chamber. We were told that this group was not against black people—only busing. When this 'anti-busing' group left City Hall, did they go beat up a school bus? No, they attacked a person. He was just walking along, and they attacked him because he had black skin."

Perhaps feeling a need to offer a different vision, the *Globe* published a letter by someone who claimed to be in City Hall Plaza at the march and said that the demonstrators were challenged "by a group of racist agitators, seven blacks and two whites, who stood on the top step of the City Hall Plaza yelling slurs at the young students peacefully making their way." No other account of the incident mentions any such group, and it is odd that the *Globe* would allow assertion to substitute for confirmation. After claiming the incident was provoked by a "communist inspired racist group," the writer went on to argue that the black community, in alliance with the media, had blown the incident out of proportion and wondered why black assaults on whites, such as "a white girl being burnt alive in Roxbury last year," received no attention.

The few letters that accused others of bias in effect underscored the point made in a letter about racism submitted by S. E. Luria, a Nobel Prize–winning physiologist at MIT. "Having known by experience what it meant to be Jewish among Nazis," Luria wrote, "I understand what it means to be black in Boston when the hoodlums roam out of control . . . Racism must be defeated not just in the schools, not just in access to various amenities, but in the structure of society, in access to jobs and to the sharing of economic and political power." Luria concluded that "it is not enough for each of us to look into his or her heart for signs of racism. We must look into our own practices, our investments, our associations, our politics to discover and unmask the poison of racism and social injustice. Where some are oppressed, is any of us free?"

The *Boston Globe* editorial on April 7 denounced the unprovoked attack as "an act of unleashed racial hatred that has been nourished by a grievous failure of leadership in the home, in the schools, from community organizations and from public officials." The *Globe* keyed especially on the actions of anti-busing activists and focused on the violation of the law, particularly truancy. "Illegal school boycotts can no longer be tolerated," the editorial stated. "Truants must be detained . . . Parades should be regulated and none should be allowed without a permit and an adequate police escort." In conclusion, the editorial reminded readers that "uncontrolled street violence in Boston has made headlines across the nation for the past two years. It is impossible to overestimate the damage it is doing to the spirit of the city, the psyche of its citizens and its reputation across the nation and throughout the world."

Mike Barnicle, the *Globe* columnist, raised the emotional and rhetorical stakes. He indicted all the parents of South Boston for claiming that race was not the reason why they opposed busing: "At City Hall Plaza, some of their children put the lie to this line of argument. At about 10:45 a man with black skin, wearing a three-piece suit, was attacked by a group of teenagers. He was beaten up for just one reason: he is a 'nigger.'" With truancy laws going unenforced, teens "roam the streets like a group of Nazi Brown Shirts." "When you take a good close look at what happened," Barnicle concluded, "it wasn't really about busing at all. It was about race, about the basics, about calling people 'niggers' and laughing as they hit the ground, noses broken and clothes spattered with blood. Theodore Landsmark was hit by a long steel pole flying the red, white, and blue flag of the United States of America. He was hit by the flag and the pole exactly eight years to the week that Martin Luther King was put into the ground in Georgia. Martin Luther King had a flag draped over him. We've come a long way."

ON APRIL 19, at 10:15 P.M., Richard Poleet, a thirty-four-year-old white man from Jamaica Plain, was driving along Harrison Street in Roxbury when black youths started throwing stones at the car. One rock crashed through the windshield, striking Poleet in the head. The driver lost control of the car and crashed into another vehicle. As a crowd assembled, some teens pulled open the door, dragged Poleet out of the car, grabbed his wallet, and beat him with rocks and fists. The victim was taken to Boston City Hospital, where he lay unconscious with a fractured, splintered skull, head and facial injuries, and internal bleeding. Police arriving on the scene said that some of the youths milling around yelled, "Let him die."

At least six detectives and four patrolmen fanned into the nearby projects in search of information. The driver of the car into which Poleet crashed described one of the attackers as six feet, 190 pounds, wearing an orange shirt and orange pants. He also said that there were girls among the group.

Within hours, police arrested Randy Lewis, age nineteen. They charged him with assault with intent to murder and armed robbery. A sixteen-year-old was also arrested and charged with assault and battery with a dangerous weapon.

As Poleet, a divorced father of two and a car mechanic at an Exxon station, lay unconscious, city officials and community leaders responded to the assault, which was perceived in only one light: as retaliation for the beating of Theodore Landsmark. A writer in the *New Republic* informed the nation that "Landsmark and Poleet are household words in Boston now. The attacks on the two men are related to one another, and they are both related to a larger train of events that, as yet, shows no sign of coming to an end."

Governor Dukakis declared that "the climate of distrust and hatred between black and white citizens of Boston must be dealt with directly and immediately . . . Talk of retribution on one side or the other must stop—it will only lead to further violence." Mayor White noted that "just as a vast majority of law-abiding citizens were outraged by what happened to Mr. Landsmark on our City Hall Plaza a very short time ago, the same individuals must feel and speak with the strongest words" against such a "despicable act." Police

Commissioner Robert diGrazia decried the "extreme political rhetoric from both blacks and whites" and said that those taking advantage of the school situation, black or white, "are not protesters. They
are thugs." William Owens predicted that "unless we immediately
work together to end the hatred and violence that has plagued our
city, the situation will only get worse as summer approaches." Mel
King insisted "that the same approach that has been taken against
white violence be taken in this and any other instance of violence."
Louise Day Hicks expressed outrage over the attack and demanded
an investigation. She also cast aspersions against King: "I wonder if
Mel King is content now that his cry, his irrational scream for retaliation [after the Landsmark incident] has been answered on the streets
of his own community with the spilling of innocent blood."

King had not called for retaliation, though at the rally the day
after the Landsmark incident there were comments offered by others
about blacks arming themselves in self-defense. As Hicks's remark
illustrated, beyond the expected denunciations of the Poleet beating,
South Boston political leaders seized on the incident to condemn
busing, attack the media, and warn of a race war in Boston.

State Senator William Bulger placed the blame "at the door-
steps of the proponents of forced busing" and indicted the media for
contributing to the hatred by "labeling opponents of forced busing as
racist and by labeling opposition to forced busing opposition to desegregation." Ray Flynn, a South Boston representative, wondered if
the media would respond to the Poleet attack "with the same outrage" as to the beating of Landsmark. But of all the spokesmen for
South Boston, James Kelly offered the most provocative, and in all
likelihood the most honest, comments. Kelly warned of an approaching race war. Describing South Boston as within a "defensive peri-

meter," he confessed that "a black is not safe in South Boston now. It wasn't always that way. Now the blacks hate the whites and the whites hate the blacks."

The editors at the *Bay State Banner*, Boston's black newspaper, lamented the assault on Poleet: "For two years we have been quite restrained despite the stoning of school buses and countless unreported assaults on innocent blacks. But the widely publicized City Hall Plaza attack on Ted Landsmark turned the tide. So they finally got to us. We were suckered in. After the brutal attack on Richard Poleet, an innocent white man driving through Roxbury, the reaction was: 'There, I told you so. Blacks are savages after all.'" The editors called for an end to all reprisals, noting that they would only serve as justification for white assaults.

In an editorial on April 21, the *Globe* editors expressed their anguish at purposeless atrocities that belied the similarities and common interests of the victims: "It didn't matter to the black hoodlums from Orchard Park . . . that their victim, an employee of a gas station, was probably as poor and downtrodden as they. It didn't matter to the white punks from Charlestown and South Boston that their victim had endeavored to find jobs for people in their neighborhoods. Only the color counts." The *Globe* again called on leaders to enforce the law, ensure safety, and encourage all citizens to express moral outrage and demand decency and respect. "Boston has so much, it has so many people of high courage and good will, that it cannot be allowed to founder in discord and disorder. The real avenging for Richard Poleet and Theodore Landsmark will come in harmony and progress, not in violence."

But there was little harmony to be found. Even the choice of a distinguished attorney as the court-appointed lawyer for Randy

Lewis rankled. Judge Elwood McKenney chose James St. Clair to represent Lewis. St. Clair was best known as special counsel to Richard Nixon during the Watergate scandal, and his appointment angered many, who wondered why such an internationally renowned figure would be chosen to defend "an unemployed black youth." McKenney defended the choice: "when the interests of the city or community are involved . . . from time to time it is our policy to appoint leading attorneys for defendants." St. Clair appeared in court with bodyguards.

The *Globe* not only published an anguished editorial but also issued a front page admission of "Error in Judgment" in its initial coverage of the stoning of Poleet, a cursory article that ran on page five. Charles Whipple, the paper's ombudsman, explained that there had been several disturbances, and only after a South Boston marshal complained that the story should be given the same coverage as the attack on Landsmark did the paper investigate the incident. Whipple observed that "mistakes were made." Reporters failed to check with editors, and editors did not call superiors in the middle of the night. It was not until the evening edition on April 20 that the story made page one. "This was poor news coverage, and it cannot be excused," concluded Whipple.

Of course, the *Globe*'s admitted errors in this case confirmed the view of anti-busing leaders that the media was hopelessly biased in its coverage of events. Whipple acknowledged receiving complaints that an intentional decision was made to bury the Poleet story. He rejected the claim, saying that the decision was not deliberate but rather a case of poor judgment where newspaper policy and practice parted ways. The *Herald American*, which had covered the story on its front page, was not so quick to let the competition slip away. A few weeks later, the paper published the comments of Harrison Salisbury, a former *New York Times* editor speaking on the CBS morning news: "The *Globe*'s play was a mistake, rather than policy, but it illustrates the delicate line which emerges when the press tries to substitute what might be called civic standards for the normal page-one standards. The effort to cool the Boston situation is laudable, but it won't work if people think the papers are trying to manipulate the news."

While Poleet remained in critical condition, political and community leaders sought ways to stem the violence and hatred. Senator Edward Brooke, the first black person to represent Massachusetts in Congress, wrote to Mayor White and offered whatever support his office could provide "in your effort to find and prosecute the thugs whose racist attack on Richard Poleet was and always will be an affront to every decent black and white citizen of Boston." Mel King held a press conference and warned that "Boston is in danger of becoming a city of random, uncontrollable violence," and he again called on the mayor "to show leadership in finding ways to end all forms of violence in the city—physical and psychological." Ted Landsmark felt especially "sickened" by the assault on Poleet and said, "I want them to know there are those of us out here ready to assist in a variety of ways."

Politicians issued statements denouncing the violence, but even these came about only after much wrangling. The twenty-seven representatives from Boston in the State House offered a statement that acknowledged that they "may disagree on many issues—including the root causes of the unrest plaguing the City of Boston." What they agreed on was that "the one thing which is killing this city more than anything else is violence." Ray Flynn and Michael Flaherty from

South Boston would not sign because the statement did not address the issue of school busing. "While we all deplore the despicable acts of violence," Flynn said, we must "recognize and admit what busing has done to race relations in Boston."

Responding to the demands that he take action, and recognizing the need to show unity in the face of racial violence, Mayor White called for an anti-violence march on Friday, April 23, through downtown Boston and culminating at City Hall Plaza. The announcement followed the cancellation of another rally, the March on Boston, organized by Maceo Dixon, coordinator of the National Student Coalition Against Racism. That march had been scheduled for Saturday and intended to support school desegregation and protest the assault on Landsmark. But in the wake of the assault on Poleet and the elevated racial tensions in the city, organizers canceled the march.

In announcing an anti-violence march, White pointed out that "each side has always had their own marches. This march isn't owned by anyone. Everyone will be invited . . . If you are against violence, come; if you are for violence you are not wanted. Non-violence will always be the symbol of a city like ours." White said the city needed to do this for itself: "The last few weeks have been a terrible time for the people of this city. A black man and a white man have been assaulted with a mindless brutality that now leaves one man fighting for his life in a hospital . . . Liberty was born in Boston and it will flourish here as long as courageous people of high moral principle are willing to speak what is in their hearts."

A *Globe* editorial, praising the idea of the march, offered a near utopian vision of what the gathering should look like and thought "it could be the most important show of faith and unity this city has ever witnessed." Imagine "what an impact it would make to see Mel King and Louise Day Hicks, Billy Bulger and Bill Owens walking together down those historic streets, not in a statement of common political purpose, but in a demonstration of common humanity."

But no sooner had the mayor made an announcement for a march to unite Boston against violence, and the newspapers endorsed it, than new violence rocked the city. On the morning of April 22, a bomb exploded at the Suffolk County Courthouse in Pemberton Square. Nineteen minutes after a phone threat received at 8:53, the explosion tore through the second-floor Probation Department, which housed criminal records. Nearly two dozen people were injured, some severely. One man's foot was blown away. Others suffered broken bones, head injuries, cuts, and contusions. A police officer said, "There was blood all over the place. I was slipping on it."

It was not surprising that everyone saw the bombing as linked to the racial violence in the city. Someone leaked word that the female caller who made the bomb threat sounded "ethnic" and made some reference to a Jackson case. The courthouse operator apparently said that she believed the caller was black; the Associated Press reported her claim as fact and then later issued a clarification saying that "there was nothing to link the bombing with recent racial strife in Boston." But link it logically, if not causally, citizens did. Robert Healy, the executive editor of the *Globe*, asserted that "the pattern of violence in Boston started with the beating of Theodore Landsmark on City Hall Plaza and escalated to the bombing."

Following the bombing, Governor Dukakis delivered a live radio and television broadcast: "These are troubled times for the City of Boston . . . A black man clubbed on City Hall Plaza. The weapon? An American flag. A white man stoned and beaten lying near death in Boston City Hospital . . . And this morning, a tragic bombing at Suffolk County Courthouse." Dukakis announced that he was creating a special law enforcement unit for the prosecution of violent crimes, and he called on citizens to work together to resolve problems peacefully and to join in the march against violence.

The courthouse bombing turned out to be the work of a revolutionary group seeking to exploit Boston's racial violence. Known as the Sam Melville–Jonathan Jackson Unit for Prison Reform, the group was a cell of the New World Liberation Front. Melville had been killed at Attica, and Jackson was the brother of the slain Black Panther George Jackson, who died in a courthouse shootout in San Francisco. The news was not reported until the day after Mayor White's march against violence. Those who gathered at the corner of Beacon and Charles streets at eleven thirty Friday morning tried to look confident, but fear filled the air, a fear known previously only by those who had participated in any of the civil rights marches in the South.

Thousands joined the march, perhaps fifteen thousand to start and as many as fifty thousand by journey's end at City Hall Plaza. Mayor White and Governor Dukakis marched. Senators Kennedy and Brooke marched. On the warm April day, some marched in shirtsleeves, including State Supreme Judicial Court Chief Justice Edward Hennessey. The president of the University of Massachusetts and the president of Harvard and seven out of the ten state college presidents marched. Businessmen, bankers, publishers, religious leaders, community organizers, students, tourists all marched. City employees had time off from work between eleven and one to attend the rally. Many businesses provided extended lunch hours. Reporters described the crowd as mostly middle class and white, though liberally sprinkled with blacks, and somewhat older and better dressed than those who had marched in other rallies in the past.

The procession against violence lasted about eighty minutes. No speeches were made, no signs allowed. At City Hall Plaza, Cardinal Humberto Medeiros prayed for help to "turn Boston from a city of crisis to a city of hope." Episcopalian bishop-elect John Colburn prayed for "perplexed and anxious" citizens to come together and strengthen "the fabric of this city." And Rabbi Roland Gittelsohn urged: "especially in this Bicentennial year, above all here in the very cradle of American freedom, may we remain true to the faith of our fathers, the faith which proclaims that, however profound our convictions, however vigorous our disputes, the way of democracy is to talk, to consider, to weigh above all, to listen even when we most strongly disagree." Led by an aide to the mayor, the vast crowd sang "God Bless America." Some held hands or linked arms. Some felt for a moment that maybe peace at last would come to Boston. And then the crowd dispersed into the afternoon sun.

For all the thousands who marched, those who stood by the side or stayed away gathered as much attention. Although most of Boston's black leaders participated, some members of the Black Legislative Caucus stayed away and met to discuss the new prosecutorial unit established by the governor. Maceo Dixon, the head of the National Student Coalition Against Racism, declared that "Mayor White will not cover up two years of morally bankrupt leadership with this march today." Mel King did not march, but he did position himself in front of the statehouse on Beacon Street, where, dressed in a blue jumpsuit and mauve hat, he chatted with marchers as they passed by. "I think this march is a good thing, and I encouraged people to march in it," he answered in response to being asked whether he was there to support the procession. "But when the prayer meeting is over," he concluded, "I think we ought to go to see the mayor and say 'What are you going to do now?'"

About the only issue on which black activists who desired de-segregation and white activists who opposed busing agreed was opposition to the mayor. Louise Day Hicks denounced the march and said, "The only march that will mean anything will be on Judge Garrity's courtroom." Raymond Flynn issued a statement saying he would not march: "good men are outraged at the escalation of violence in the city, wise men will recognize the failure of busing and courageous men will admit the mistakes of two years and resolve to do something about them." "Forced busing is a cancer on the city of Boston," said Jim Kelly, "and this march is putting a Band-Aid on a cancer." Councilman John Kerrigan told Mayor White, "While I deplore the violence that forced busing has brought to our city, I cannot in good conscience join you in marching with those who brought this holocaust about."

Whatever hope the procession against violence gave Boston dissipated in the recognition that, in the words of *Globe* columnist Jeremiah Murphy, "The Wrong People Were There." What he meant was that the people relevant to reducing the crisis were not there. Murphy's column hit hard:

> Where was Rep. Ray Flynn from South Boston and Louise Day Hicks and City Councilman Albert L. O'Neil? And where was Jimmy Kelly of the South Boston Information Service and those teenagers who march along clapping and chanting over and over 'Here We Go, Southie, Here We Go?' . . .
>
> And where was NAACP Pres. Tom Atkins and Ken

Guscott and Rep. Doris Bunte? They are black leaders and have militantly supported busing in Boston. They were not marching in the parade.

And what about the young guys who pass the July nights sitting around the D Street Project in Southie and listening to the anti-busing hatred voiced by the adults? . . . Their counterparts at the misnamed Orchard Park housing project in Roxbury were not there, and the absence of both groups perhaps is the greatest tragedy, because if violence comes again it probably will start with these young men . . .

School busing will not be solved by the people who marched in that parade. The personalities involved were not present, so the tragedy will continue because the mutual hatred goes too deep.

Several days after the march, two fifteen-year-olds appeared in juvenile court and were found delinquent for assault and battery on Ted Landsmark "by means of a dangerous weapon—a shod foot." The judge placed both on probation until they reached age eighteen. The judge also took the unusual step of recommending that the teens write a public letter of apology. The attorney representing one of the assailants said that the defendants had both apologized to Landsmark in open court, and that he would approve the issuance of a public letter that warned others of the dangers of violent acts. At a separate arraignment in Suffolk Superior Court, Edward Irvin and Joseph Rakes, charged with kicking the victim and assaulting Landsmark with a flagpole, pleaded not guilty. They would later be convicted of assault and battery and of assault with a dangerous weapon.

On May 5, the two juveniles, found guilty and placed on

probation, issued a public statement: "We hope that the people of Boston, in particular the young people both black and white, can learn by our experience that acts of violence serve no meaningful purpose and can only lead to unnecessary grief and mental anguish to both themselves and their families . . . We apologized personally to Mr. Landsmark in court. He accepted our apology. Unfortunately, we realize that the apology cannot wipe out the incident."

The apology, written by the lawyers, did not satisfy everyone. One writer to the *Globe* decried probation as far too lenient and evidence of a general permissiveness in society. It served as no deterrent, she claimed, and, in a way, further highlighted the racism of differential treatment for white and black defendants. Pointing out that Poleet's assailant was being held on bail of twenty-five thousand dollars for an assault that, while certainly more severe, was not dramatically different from the Landsmark case, she concluded that "the difference in the treatment of these white and black criminals could cause more racial strife."

On June 23, the Mayor's Committee on Violence presented their report to Mayor White. An ad hoc committee created to study the causes of racial violence in the city, the group had frank conversations with leaders from all constituencies in the struggle over busing and desegregation. Their report was balanced and fair and concluded that "we are witnessing a struggle between whites and blacks who are angry, bitter and frustrated because of poverty, unemployment, poor housing, inferior education, and court-ordered busing." The committee found problems with communication and leadership and faulted the massive police presence that incited opposition. But given the intractability of the problems that they found ("a depressed city with depressed communities," they said), they could offer little but bromides and encouragement. The might of Boston as "a city of neighborhoods" is strongest, they attested, when "these diverse neighborhoods use their strengths and sense of pride to pull together to meet a common enemy." Alluding to the Revolution, the report concluded that "it is true of the neighborhoods of Boston today, as it was of the thirteen colonies two hundred years ago, that we must all hang together or we will all hang separately."

The city of Boston tried to look ahead to the end of the school year and the July 4 celebrations. But the Landsmark incident and other episodes of racial violence left most thinking Americans singing what the editors at *Ebony* called "the Bicentennial Blues." "We cannot celebrate the country or its technological achievements," they insisted, "if we do not confront the meaning of the Landsmark incident and what we have not done and must do to be worthy of the Revolutionary heritage . . . The Bicentennial Blues . . . is rooted in the belief that we should use this occasion to reverse the drift toward division and disaster. The Bicentennial Blues is based, moreover, on a belief that incidents like the Boston attack indicate that we are in serious trouble as a people, and that nothing short of great moral leadership will save us."

After all the speeches, statements, letters, editorials, debates, investigations, reports, indictments, marches, and prayers, one writer was left only with sarcasm as a means of combating the misery. The schools, he said, are so broken they cannot even teach common sense: "Those white kids who beat up the black lawyer on the steps of City Hall. Not only did they use an American flag, but they did it in front of cameras."

CHAPTER 6

REVERBERATIONS

FOR THE TWO months following the incident at City Hall Plaza, whenever Stanley Forman covered an event in South Boston, pro-testers pointed him out and shouted, "He's the one, that's him who took the picture." Once, at a fire, he had to be escorted to safety. "In Southie, I was shit because of the picture," he recalls. The opponents of busing knew he had taken the photograph, and they knew how much damage it had done to their cause. Forman's photograph did not end the resistance to busing, but it marked a turning point from which the movement could not recover. However strenuously the anti-busing movement emphasized issues other than race, the photo-graph shattered the protesters' claim that racism did not animate their cause and that they were patriotic Americans fighting for their liberties. The photograph had seared itself into the collective mem-ory of the city and installed itself in the imagination of both blacks and whites.

Stanley Forman was in Amsterdam in late April 1976, accept-ing the World Press Photo Award for his fire escape photos from a year before, when he learned that he had also won the Pulitzer Prize for spot news photography. There was a party in the *Herald* offices on May 3 when the official announcement came. He received telegrams and phone calls congratulating him. He left the celebration early to get to the Garden for the Bruins-Flyers game. And then, the next day, he was back to work. He covered a bomb threat, went to a protest by the Amalgamated Clothing Workers, and called it a day.

Already, there was buzz that his flag photograph would win a second Pulitzer and carry off every other top award. Dave O'Brian, a former *Record American* reporter and now media columnist for the *Boston Phoenix*, came to the defense of his former colleague who was the target of barbs from jealous newsmen:

> So *Herald American* photographer Stan Forman (who, the paper tells us, still eats his breakfast and walks his dog just as if nothing had happened) won the big one. Having copped a Pulitzer Prize for his stunning photo sequence of 20-year-old Diane Bryant falling to her death after the collapse of a Back Bay fire escape, Forman, at the tender age of 30, is now a bona fide star.
>
> Of course, the office cynics were saying for a while that for Forman it would surely be all downhill from here. The pictures were great, the cynics conceded, but only because Forman just happened, as they say, to be "in the right place at the right time." And since he was using a motorized camera, they were saying, it didn't even take much skill to get those admittedly terrific shots.
>
> But I wonder what they are saying now that Stan Forman is a serious candidate for a 1977 Pulitzer. Indeed, Forman's shot of an anti-busing demonstrator assaulting black lawyer Theodore Landsmark with the American flag may, in terms of its obvious symbolism, be an even greater photograph than this year's winner. Again, of course, Forman was lucky. But this time he was one of many who were snapping their shutters as the

Landsmark attack occurred and yet was the only photographer to come away with the photo of the event. So you begin to wonder if being "in the right place at the right time" might be the result of more than just luck.

This time around, Forman kept the presentation simple, submitting only *The Soiling of Old Glory* as a single, simply mounted image. A year later he learned that he had won a second consecutive Pulitzer Prize for spot news photography.

In Boston, one African American artist responded to the image almost immediately in the only way he knew how, with three large (two were 48"×70" and one 70"×48") acrylic works depicting the assault. Dana Chandler grew up in Roxbury and graduated from the Massachusetts College of Art in 1967. He became active in the civil rights movement and involved with Artists Against the War. Chandler began teaching at Simmons College in 1971 and in 1974 had studio space and taught at Northeastern University, where he established the African American Master Artists-in-Residency Program. In 1976, Northeastern's art gallery featured Chandler's exhibition "If the Shoe Fits, Hear It." Shortly after the exhibition closed on April 2, Chandler, like everyone else in Boston, saw Forman's photograph. By December he had completed his canvases.

Chandler's brightly colored works used the flag as a motif in depicting three moments: the original assault, the attack with the flag, and a portrait of Landsmark afterward. It is clear from pictures taken at an unveiling of the work at Northeastern, an event attended by Landsmark, that Chandler consulted several of Forman's photographs. The pictures on the bulletin board to the right are in reverse chronological order and show Landsmark immedi-

Dana Chandler, Landsmark paintings, 1976 (NORTHEASTERN
UNIVERSITY ARCHIVES AND SPECIAL COLLECTIONS)

ately after the attack, the assault with the flag, and the beating
prior to the flag's arrival. Newspaper accounts of the assault are
also posted.

The paintings are three canvases that flow together. In choosing to execute a triptych, Chandler was tying his subject to the tradition of Christian art, which often featured three hinged panels that
depicted the Crucifixion. In the first panel, the flag unfurls like the
wings of a predator as Landsmark is kicked and stomped. He falls
to the pavement, which Chandler painted red, green, and black, the
colors of the black nationalist flag first adopted in 1920 and put to

Dana Chandler, Landsmark paintings, 1976 (NORTHEASTERN
UNIVERSITY ARCHIVES AND SPECIAL COLLECTIONS)

various uses by advocates of black and African liberation since. It is
possible that the foreground figure on the right expresses horror,
but no help is forthcoming. In the third panel, that figure now
faces the viewer. Unlike in the photograph, Landsmark is eyeing his
attacker. Also unlike in the photograph, the man holding him from
behind is also beating him. In both panels, hands are central elements: fists fly and fingers curl. Landsmark uses his hands to steady
himself, but his black hand, made prominent against the white
stripe, will not stop the flag from reaching its target. In the portrait
of Landsmark that is the middle panel, his face is bandaged with the
flag's stars. He glares at us, enraged. The white stripe of the flag flows
across the three panels, tying them together. The event, Chandler
said, proved "that the American flag is in fact a weapon against black
people."

For one black family, the incident and photograph forever shaped a child's identity. Janus Adams, journalist, historian, producer, and, it so happens, Ted Landsmark's cousin, recalled the impact of the image on her daughter, who was only in nursery school at the time of the incident, but who later said that the picture marked her racial awakening. Adams recounts what her daughter told her: "That incident made me understand there was something beyond being mean spirited. It was something so random. There was no reason for it. He [Landsmark] didn't do anything to anybody. A lot of people don't have that concept of hatred just for the sake of hatred, but it existed for us as black children. In America . . . black people and white people walk on the same road but on different sides of a wall. To us race is something we don't have the privilege of ignoring. I learned young to look beyond what things seem to be. There is a reason why people get attacked for nothing." To this day, Adams recalled in 2004, "our family is stabbed to its core when that photo crops up."

We might expect that Forman's photograph would haunt the black community, but its impact also reached deep into South Boston itself. Michael Patrick MacDonald grew up in the Old Colony projects, and his memoir, *All Souls: A Family Story from Southie*, is a searing account of life in the neighborhood. McDonald's mother saw the photograph on the front page of the *Herald American* and said, about her neighbor taking aim with the American flag, "What a vicious son of a bitch." "Busing is a horror," she said, "but this is no way to fight for it. People like that are making us all look bad."

MacDonald's account continues, and it provides a different perspective on the anti-busing movement:

[Ma] said she was starting to think that some politicians in Southie were almost as bad as Judge Garrity himself. She thought they might be stirring things up in the drugged-out minds of people like the teenager in the *Herald*. "And the kids are the ones suffering," she said. "Especially the ones who can't get into the parochial school with the seats filling up and the tuitions being raised." She said she felt she was kicked in the stomach every time she heard Jimmy Kelly talking about niggers this and niggers that at the Information Center where she'd been volunteering. She said she couldn't get used to that word, no matter how much she hated the busing. Then there were the South Boston Marshalls, the militant group connected to the Information Center. We all wanted to stop the busing, but sometimes it was confusing. One day you'd be clapping and cheering the inspirational words of Louise Day Hicks and Senator Billy Bulger, and the next day you'd see the blood on the news, black and white people's blood. And here was a black man being beaten with the American flag on the national news.

MacDonald's mother was not alone in her feelings, and in elections the following year voters turned away from anti-busing militants. Both Louise Day Hicks and John Kerrigan lost their City Council seats. Elvira "Pixie" Palladino, a firebrand from East Boston and an ally of Kerrigan who split with Hicks over tactics, had been elected to the School Committee in 1975 but now lost her seat. A moderate, Kathleen Sullivan, received the most votes for the committee. But even more remarkable, John O'Bryant was elected. His last name may have sounded Irish, but O'Bryant was black, and he became the first black to be elected to the School Committee in a citywide election.

The tensions in the schools seemed to have abated as well. "Truce in Boston," declared *Time* about opening day in September 1976. No helicopters; no sharpshooters; just pockets of protesters. Eighteen months later, a reporter visited South Boston High School and found that the "open hatred and fear has finally dissipated" and that "only a lingering uneasiness" remained. A black student said, "It's a lot better than it was before." A white student admitted that coming to school was better than standing on the street corner. Teachers had gotten control of the corridors, where so much mischief took place in 1974 and 1975, and regained an enthusiasm for teaching in a more relaxed atmosphere. "Desegregation did not carry with it the end to effective and solid education," said one teacher. "In many respects it meant the beginning of it."

The report also pointed out that there were few students in the classrooms and that this fact, as much as anything else, explained the easing of tensions. Between 1974 and 1977, the percentage of white students in the Boston school system declined from 55 percent to 42 percent. By 1980, it was down to 35 percent, and by 1987, 26 percent. Rather than accept desegregation, the whites who were able to left the system—for parochial schools, for the suburbs if they could afford it, for no schooling at all. A debate over "white flight" emerged, a debate that was in effect a referendum on the consequences of busing. Supporters of busing argued against a correlation between busing and movement to the suburbs by white families. They citied studies by political scientists and sociologists who claimed to find "little or no significant white flight, even when [busing] is court ordered and implemented in large cities." But the preponderance of the evidence seemed to support the reality of white flight in situations such as Boston's: court-ordered busing of whites as well as blacks, a large district, high black enrollments, and available white suburbs. Moreover, there was anticipatory flight as many whites left before desegregation plans took effect. However much supporters of desegregation wished it not to be true, in Boston, according to Ronald Formisano, "white flight could account for at least half of the total white loss from the schools during 1974–1980."

Responding to the easing of tensions, Garrity relinquished control of the schools, first giving the responsibility for compliance with the court's order to the state board of education and then, in September 1985, returning authority over the educational system to the School Committee. By then, there was a new mayor in Boston, a symbol of a new urban politics that would seek to revitalize Boston and turn the city around. Less than a decade before his election in 1983, it would have been unimaginable that an Irishman from South Boston, an opponent of busing, could have become mayor. But the mayoral race between Ray Flynn, the victor, and Mel King, the black activist and former legislator who himself ran a vigorous and engaging campaign that garnered both white and black support, reenergized a defeated city. Voters believed, according to the *New York Times,* that "after years of racial strife and neglect of the city's neighborhoods, the city is changing for the better."

Flynn, the son of Irish immigrants, graduated from South Boston High School in 1958, and after attending Providence College he returned to South Boston and was elected a state representative in 1968. He was as virulently opposed to busing as Louise Day Hicks and William Bulger, but he chose a more moderate path when he refused to sign the Declaration of Clarification and focused his attention more on the topic of the police presence in South Boston and support for a biracial parents' advisory council than on the racial fault line of desegregation. Bulger later said that Flynn had a "certain fluidity of principle . . . and could read the wind like a wolf." By 1983, the sail was up for the wind of moderation, and it swept Flynn into the mayor's office. Once there, he never slowed, stopping on his runs to play basketball with black kids in Roxbury, or giving McDonald's gift certificates to sanitation workers at Kenmore Square, or visiting the cafeteria at South Boston High School, where the students cheered. In his inauguration speech, he invoked Lincoln: "Boston has for too long been a house divided against itself. We have endured the worst sort of polarization and confrontation, but our resolve now is to bind old wounds, put the memories behind us, and carry worthwhile lessons into the future . . . This is a time for hating the violence and discord of the past. It is a time for loving the city and all its people."

Less than two years after Flynn's election, Boston paused to look back on the tumultuous events of the seventies when J. Anthony Lukas published *Common Ground: A Turbulent Decade in the Lives of Three American Families*. It was seeing Forman's photograph that led Lukas to start his project. "In that single image he saw his beloved Boston being torn asunder," recalled the journalist Samuel Freedman. Seven years in the research and writing, Lukas's book brought to life the struggles of desegregation by focusing on three representative families: the Divers, a liberal suburban Yankee family; the McGoffs, Irish Americans from Charlestown; and the Twymons, a widowed black woman and her six children. Through their stories, and the stories of dozens of others, Lukas painted a stunning, textured portrait of Boston in crisis. He wrote breathlessly and with deep empathy for his subjects, and in Boston's story he found not only himself but also a larger story: "I believe that what happened in

Boston was not a random series of events but the acting out of the burden of American history."

On September 28, 1985, a town meeting on race and class, organized in conjunction with the publication of *Common Ground*, drew five hundred people to the Kennedy Library on a Saturday night. The many panelists and commentators covered the spectrum of the busing crisis: Paul Parks, former Massachusetts secretary of education; Robert Kiley, former deputy mayor; Thomas Winship, former *Globe* editor; assorted professors, ministers, parents, and activists. At one point, Elvira "Pixie" Palladino spoke, and her anger still flashed. She denounced forced busing as a class issue and lamented how few anti-busing representatives were at the forum. "The only common ground we're ever going to have is that we love our kids," she declared. Knowing how the largely white, middle-class, liberal crowd must have felt about her, she asked, "How many of you are going to love me, no matter what color I am?" From the audience, Wayne Twymon, who had been bused to Brighton High School, said softly, "Pixie, I do love you."

Ted Landsmark was also one of the panelists. Landsmark had left the law to pursue his other passion, art education. Now dean of graduate and continuing education at the Massachusetts College of Art, Landsmark was one of the leading black educators in the state. "I suppose for the rest of my life I'll always be thought of in the context of a photograph," he said, and then he drew a laugh when he commented on how he was an amateur photographer and, although he obviously didn't take the picture, he felt as if he too had won a Pulitzer. Landsmark pointed out that his only involvement in education issues came indirectly as a result of the photograph and that his work had been related to affirmative action in the workplace.

The importance of the publication of Lukas's book, he thought, was not so much that it made Bostonians look back as that it encouraged them to think ahead about "what it is we want to do at this point." The most significant common ground, he said, "is that we have committed ourselves to being in Boston for the long haul and have made a basic and fundamental commitment to Boston."

What disturbed him most was the composition of the room. "I don't know that I often agree with Pixie," he remarked, "but there is one thing she says that really does strike me, and that is that there are some people who have been heavily involved in this whole thing who aren't here." He lamented that "the number of people of color is very small," and he speculated about the reasons why they weren't at the town hall and maybe had given up on Boston completely. Whenever he traveled, friends said to him, "Oh yeah, Boston, you're still there? That city is really racist."

Racist or not, Landsmark said, it seemed clear that Boston had limited opportunities for blacks to grow personally and professionally. Few served on corporate boards of banks or insurance companies; few had art exhibitions of their own. "How many of you know a black realtor in this town?" he asked. What was needed was for the private sector to respond and provide opportunities— and role models—not only for black children but for white children as well. He reminded the group that nearly ten years earlier, in the aftermath of the assault, he had remarked that "the chances of any of the kids who attacked me ending up on a major corporate board in Boston are as slim as any black kid ending up on a board." Landsmark made the same point as Palladino: "it's a matter of class that we are looking at." And it was up to the people in that room not to celebrate having survived the turmoil of the seventies but to make progress for the future by helping to open up opportunities and possibilities.

In March 1990, emotions again flared over *Common Ground*, which had been adapted into a two-part made-for-television movie. The film was long and melodramatic, and it offered stereotypes where Lukas had provided nuance. It also distorted events, none more so than the assault on Landsmark. In the movie, Landsmark is attacked not by students but by parents. He is beaten until he is nearly unconscious. The man carrying the flag is wearing a Boston Celtics jacket, and he lines up the staff, taking careful aim. The camera is located behind the victim, placing the viewer in the position of Landsmark as the staff is thrust into his face. Landsmark is left lying unconscious on the ground.

While the film version may have sketched the essence of the larger conflict over busing, no one at a screening in Boston approved its more sensationalistic aspects. Palladino called it "a piece of pornography," and Jim Kelly told the film's producer, "You don't know what you are talking about." Landsmark thought the film might generate "a lot of anger and anxiety." Always thinking about community, he suggested that the producers donate some of their profit to the city "to further the healing process that is going to be sorely tested by this film."

That healing process hadn't yet reached Landsmark's flag-wielding assailant from 1976. Joseph Rakes found himself running out of hope. The photograph may have made him a momentary hero among his least reflective friends, but very quickly he felt only despair. In 2001, Thomas Farragher, a *Boston Globe* reporter, spoke to Rakes and two of his brothers. It was the first time Rakes had spoken to the press about the incident. One of his brothers said that after the photograph appeared, "he went into a shell . . . He thought every-body was looking at him. He didn't want to talk about it. It was a bad time in his life. Everybody knew him as the 'flag kid.' And that can wear on you year after year. He hated it." Joseph Rakes said that he was in a state of "blind anger" over busing: when it started, "it was 'You can't have half your friends'—that's the way it was put towards us. They took half the boys and girls I grew up with and said, 'You're going to school on the other side of town.' Nobody understood it at 15." He explained to Farragher, "There was no thinking whatsoever. It was more rage than anything. I didn't know until it was over what had happened. I remember turning and running. I mean, when you think about it, that Stanley Forman had a quick finger."

Essentially, Rakes kept running. He graduated in 1977 and bounced around in different minimum-wage jobs. In 1983, he got into a fight with Thomas Dooley, who was dating Rakes's sister. He smashed Dooley over the head with a lead pipe. Ten days later, Dooley died, but not before identifying Rakes, who fled. For five years, Rakes ran, rumored to be in Florida and the Bahamas. In 1988, he finally turned himself in, but by then evidence and witnesses had disap-peared. The prosecution's case had become stale, and first-degree murder charges were dropped. Rakes started a construction job, mar-ried a South Boston girl, and moved north of Boston. When Farra-gher spoke to him in 2001, he was working on Boston's Big Dig. Rakes lamented the loss of Southie—of close family ties and kinship networks and ethnic loyalties. Now, he said, it was simply South Bos-ton. But one artifact from his youth remained in his possession: the flag he carried that day sat folded in a cabinet at home.

As Rakes tried to reassemble his life, the American flag again became a national flashpoint. In 1989, a divided Supreme Court issued its decision in *Texas v. Johnson*. The case stemmed from an incident at the 1984 Republican National Convention in Dallas. Gregory Lee Johnson, a member of the Revolutionary Communist Youth Brigade, a radical Maoist organization, participated in a political demonstration in protest of the renomination of Ronald Reagan and corporate businesses in Dallas. The rowdy protesters shrieked obscenities, disrupted businesses, and committed minor acts of vandalism, including taking a flag from outside a bank. When they reached Dallas City Hall, Johnson took out the flag, poured kerosene on it, and set it ablaze. Protesters chanted, "America, the red, white, and blue / we spit on you."

Johnson was charged with violating a Texas flag-desecration law passed in 1973. He was convicted, and the conviction was upheld by the state court of appeals. The Texas Court of Criminal Appeals, however, reversed the conviction, and the U.S. Supreme Court affirmed that decision. Writing for a 5–4 majority, Justice William J. Brennan argued that Johnson's actions "were symbolic speech protected by the First Amendment . . . The expressive, overtly political nature of this conduct was both intentional and overwhelmingly apparent." Rejecting Texas's argument that desecration of the flag is a crime because it destroys a "symbol of nationhood and national unity," the Court held that "if there is a bedrock principle underlying the First Amendment, it is that the government may not prohibit the expression of an idea simply because society finds the idea itself offensive or disagreeable . . . The way to preserve the flag's special role," Brennan concluded, "is not to punish those who feel differently about these matters. It is to persuade them that they are wrong."

In his dissent, joined by Justices Byron White and Sandra Day O'Connor, Chief Justice William Rehnquist was not happy. He reviewed the history of the flag and then admonished his brethren for concluding the majority opinion with "a regrettably patronizing civics lecture." "Surely one of the high purposes of a democratic society," argued Rehnquist, "is to legislate against conduct that is regarded as evil and profoundly offensive to the majority of people—whether it be murder, embezzlement, pollution, or flag burning."

The Court's decision was met with what *Newsweek* called "stunned outrage." The Senate, in a 97–3 resolution, expressed "profound disappointment" with the decision. The House, in a 411–5 vote, expressed "profound concern." Politicians scrambled to outdo one another in denouncing flag burning and the Court's decision. One Republican congressman proclaimed that "probably no Supreme Court decision in our history since the infamous Dred Scott decision of 1857 has elicited such a spontaneous outburst of rage, anger and sadness on the part of the American people." Congress quickly passed a new Flag Protection Act, but the Supreme Court struck it down. Long before that decision, President George H. W. Bush, standing before the Iwo Jima Memorial, called for a constitutional amendment banning flag desecration, and polls showed that most Americans supported him.

In 1989, a Senate vote on a constitutional amendment ("The Congress and the States shall have the power to prohibit the physical desecration of the flag of the United States") fell short by fifteen votes of the two-thirds majority needed. The amendment returned again in 1995 and has been passed by the House and rejected by the Senate in every Congress since (though in 2006 it failed by only one vote in the Senate). It was easy to mock the absurdity of the amendment, and an essayist at *Time* spoke for most pundits when he wondered, "If there is only one official U.S. flag, would it be permissible to burn an unofficial one—say, an obsolete model with 48 stars? . . . What about little lapel pins or cuff links with flags on them? What if somebody publicly stomped a piece of such jewelry? . . . Should a law protecting the flag also protect homemade facsimiles of the flag? Is a crayon drawing of the flag a flag? Besides burning, what would constitute the 'physical' desecration some of our political leaders emphasize they hope to outlaw? Does that include obscenely wagging a finger at a flag? Sticking out one's tongue at the flag? Thumbing a nose at the flag? What if some miscreant mooned the flag? Or stuck pins in the flag—in public?" However inventive the scenarios imagined by commentators (electrocuting someone who had a flag tattoo), their point about the ambiguity of the amendment, not to mention its collision with the First Amendment, might be well taken by liberals, but the rising tide of moral conservatives in America meant that most politicians feared opposing the amendment and being branded as unpatriotic.

Controversies over depiction of the flag in art further fueled the cries for a constitutional amendment and help account for the return of the amendment in 1995. In 1989, a conceptual artist, Dread Scott, displayed his work *What Is the Proper Way to Display a U.S. Flag?* at an exhibition at the School of the Art Institute of Chicago. Scott, raised in Chicago's Hyde Park, describes himself as making "revolutionary art to propel history forward." *What Is the Proper Way* consists of several parts: a mounted photograph that has the title of the work and shows a collage of flag-draped coffins and South Korean students burning the American flag and holding signs (YANKEE GO HOME SON OF BITCH), a mounted shelf below the photograph with a blank book and pen, and a 3'×5' flag spread on the ground. Viewers were encouraged to write comments in the book, which would require them to stand on the flag as they did so. One writer said Scott

Dread Scott, What Is the Proper Way to Display a U.S. Flag?, *1989*
(COURTESY DREAD SCOTT)

should be shot; one wrote, "Let it burn"; one denounced the flag as a
racist symbol of an oppressive regime; another called Scott an "ass-
hole"; and one entry thanked the artist: "It does hurt me to see the
flag on the ground being stepped on. Yet now after days have passed,
I have realized that this is the ultimate form of patriotism. Our

country is so strong in believing what it stands for that we would allow you to do this. You have made me really think about my own
patriotism, which has grown stronger."

The installation elicited a storm of protest. Veterans' groups
marched outside, and when they entered the exhibition they picked
the flag up off the floor, only to have the guards restore it to its intended position. Police threatened to arrest anyone who stood on the
flag. The gallery received bomb threats, and Scott received death
threats. Politicians tried everything to close down the exhibition. A
lawsuit failed when a judge ruled that "this exhibition is as much an
invitation to think about the flag as it is an invitation to step on it."
President Bush called the work "disgraceful," and the debate over
passage of the Flag Protection Act included references to "the so-
called 'artist' who has invited trampling on the flag."

In 1994, Scott's piece was one of dozens, along with works by
Jasper Johns, Kate Millett, Robert Mapplethorpe, Faith Ringgold,
and many others, featured in an exhibition titled "Old Glory: The
American Flag in Contemporary Art." Inspired in part by the 1989
debate over flag desecration, curator David Rubin surveyed artistic
representations of the flag primarily from the 1960s, '70s, and '80s.
In Cleveland, where the exhibit opened, "Old Glory" received critical reviews, and when the show moved to Arizona in 1996, once
again it was met with protest. Veterans repeatedly grabbed the flag
out of the toilet in Kate Millett's piece and off of the floor in Scott's,
and they marched outside in opposition. Politicians denounced the
show and threatened to cut off all funding to the Phoenix Art Museum. Although in the second half of the twentieth century artists
and the culture at large had desacralized the flag as a symbol of patriotism and nationalism, representations of Old Glory continued to

evoke powerful emotions. The idea of disrespecting the flag, especially to cultural conservatives and military veterans, seemed treasonous. At the same time, many Americans wondered whether they were included in the social compact signified by Old Glory, and whether they could continue unequivocally to support the direction of the country. Patriotism in the late 1980s and the 1990s became the focus of a symbolic politics that seemed to eschew tackling deeper issues of economic disparity and social injustice. Americans had always enlisted the flag to give legitimacy to their cause, to claim membership in the nation, but now all too often they were being asked to "rally around the flag" (a phrase first sung during the Civil War) simply for the flag's sake.

And then came 9/11. In the outpouring of national feeling after the terrorist attack, flags were everywhere, waved by everyone. Even those who disdained the flag took newspaper reproductions and taped them to their windows. One writer spoke for many when he said, "I love Old Glory. I just wonder if I can take it back from the creeps who've waved it all my life." Writing in *Salon* on September 18, 2001, King Kaufman captured the tension: "For most of my life, the American flag has been the cultural property of people I can't stand: right-wingers, jingoists, know-nothing zealots. It's something that hypocritical politicians wrap themselves in. It's something that certain legislators would make it a crime to burn—a position that's an assault on the very freedom that the flag represents . . . But I also love the flag. Seeing it stirs something in me, even when I'm mad at it, or disagree with those who wave it. I am, after all, an American, and despite being opposed to every single military adventure this nation has undertaken in my lifetime, I'm a patriotic one at that."

Michael Moore, a documentary filmmaker who often clashed with conservatives, agreed. "For too long now," he argued, "we have abandoned our flag to those who see it as a symbol of war and dominance, as a way to crush dissent at home . . . Those who absconded with our flag now use it as a weapon against those who question America's course. They remind me of that famous 1976 photo of an anti-busing demonstrator in Boston thrusting a large American flag on a pole into the stomach of the first black man he encountered. These so-called patriots hold the flag tightly in their grip and, in a threatening pose, demand that no one ask questions . . . I think it's time for those of us who love this country—and everything it should stand for—to reclaim our flag from those who would use it to crush rights and freedoms, both here at home and overseas."

Moore was writing in 2004, in opposition to the Patriot Act, which gave the federal government unprecedented powers to infringe on civil liberties in the interest of national security. By then, a photograph taken on 9/11 had given new life to Old Glory. Thomas Franklin, of the *Bergen Record*, spent most of that day at the riverfront by Jersey City, shooting pictures of the smoldering buildings before their collapse and of survivors as they got off the tugboats carrying them to safety from lower Manhattan. Police kept stopping him, even threatening to arrest him, but he kept going. At some point, he was pushed and his camera slammed into a light pole. The camera jammed, and he lost all the pictures he shot that morning.

In late afternoon, he managed to hitch a ride across the Hudson. At the scene, he worked his way toward ground zero. He did not even know if his camera was functioning correctly, but he kept on taking pictures. Late in the afternoon, he was standing beneath what had been an elevated walkway and saw the firefighters off in the distance preparing to raise the flag. He was more than 150 yards away, shooting with a long lens that collapsed the distance between the men and the rubble behind them. He took twenty-three shots and then, nervous about losing the image, removed the photo card from his digital camera and placed it in his pocket. From a hotel, he transmitted two pictures to his office. The photograph, the fourteenth shot of the sequence, taken at 5:01 P.M., appeared on the front page of the *Bergen Record* the next day, and soon was seen around the world.

Old Glory Raised at New York's World Trade Center is what some called the photo. Franklin calls it *Flag Raising at Ground Zero*. The photograph redeemed the flag from the ambiguity of the previous decades and restored to it a luster not envisioned since Joe Rosenthal's photograph. Franklin immediately made the connection: "As soon as I shot it," he said, "I realized the similarity to the famous image of Marines raising the flag at Iwo Jima." Franklin's photo is monumental, a study in contrasts. The red, white, and blue puncture the sea of gray destruction; the firefighters' delicate hands are set against sharp, twisted steel; the eyes look up at a moment when all has come crashing down. There is a religious sensibility to the image, the twisted steel seeming to form a cathedral and suggesting the shape of a cross. One can tell a compelling story about America from the three great news photographs that feature Old Glory: Joe Rosenthal's, Stanley Forman's, and Tom Franklin's. The story would be about triumphant nationalism in World War II, deep-rooted hatred at the time of the Bicentennial, and stubborn courage in the face of catastrophe in the new millennium.

Tom Franklin, Flag Raising at Ground Zero, *2001* (COURTESY TOM
FRANKLIN AND THE *BERGEN RECORD*)

Eric Gay, Milvertha Hendricks, *2005* (ASSOCIATED PRESS)

Or consider a different story suggested by a different sequence of images: James Karales's photograph of a civil rights protester in 1965, Stanley's Forman's picture, and an image taken by Eric Gay on September 1, 2005. Gay made it to the French Quarter in New Orleans just as Hurricane Katrina reached Category 5. Thousands of residents, mainly black, could not evacuate, and they congregated at the Convention Center. There was no food or water or electricity or emergency service, but they kept coming because they had nowhere else to go, and help, days after the storm hit, still had not arrived. Milvertha Hendricks, age eighty-four, was one of hundreds who sat outside in the rain. In Gay's photograph, the American flag provides her only shelter. She stares ahead, but there is no life in her eyes. Her brow is furrowed; her lips are pressed tightly together. The fingers of her right hand dangle beneath a red stripe of the flag, which reaches back to cover a few others. The flag is her mourning shawl. Whatever promises had been made to her by the civil rights movement of the 1960s had been broken.

ON 9/11, STANLEY Forman jumped into his van and headed toward New York. In doing so, he was following the instinct of every photojournalist within driving distance. He had his cameras loaded and ready, but before he traveled very far down Interstate 95, he got a call to turn around and head to Logan Airport. Information was coming in that one or two of the hijacked planes originated in Boston, and his editors sent him to Logan to cover the story. He got the only images of the car the hijackers used, and of seats being taken off of a connecting flight for investigation. But not being able to get to New York, for what one writer has called "the most widely observed and photographed breaking news event in human history," broke his heart.

Covering the story at Logan Airport meant shooting moving images. In 1983, Forman left still photography for videography when he joined WCVB in Boston. The previous year the Hearst Corporation had sold the *Herald American* to Rupert Murdoch, and the paper became a tabloid, the *Boston Herald*. Forman decided it was time for a change. He'd had a chance a few years earlier, after winning his second Pulitzer, to move to the *New York Times*. After all, he was one of the premier photojournalists in the country, so much so that Nikon took out an ad in *News Photographer* in 1978 that showed his work and read, "Right now Stan Forman is cruising the streets of Boston waiting for his radio to crackle into life. The next call could send him and his Nikon cameras off to win a third Pulitzer Prize." (The staff photographers of the *Herald American* won the Pulitzer Prize in 1979 for coverage of the blizzard of 1978. Technically, Forman had won a third Pulitzer, though he does not count it because he was laid up with a broken leg.)

When the *New York Times* called, he went down for an interview. He had a nice lunch at Toots Shor's and enjoyed his visit, but he never really considered making the change. An item in the gossip pages suggesting that the *Times* was wooing him earned Forman a raise, and he stayed at the *Herald American*. He has no regrets. The *Times* was not for him, and the self-described "home boy" was not about to leave Boston.

The switch to video excited him. At age thirty-eight, Forman took it as a challenge and felt revitalized by the move. He also did not think of the shift from still to moving images as all that remarkable. "It was the same job with a different tool," he says. Besides, he had no delusions about his gifts. He had been "another mediocre photographer that made a great picture and suddenly became non-mediocre." Time and again Forman has said he is not a real photographer and uses Eddie Adams, the Vietnam War photojournalist, as a comparison. One time he was on a trip with Adams and other photographers. Everyone took a shot of a guy diving off a boat. Adams's vision stood out—his picture was at an angle, whereas Forman's was straight down. Adams could "see" in a certain way that Forman feels he could not. Maybe the difference was between news photography and photojournalism, a term Forman does not use. "I shoot news," he declares. "If it is moving I'm going to get it."

If Forman is too self-effacing (in 1980 he received the highest award given by the National Press Photographers Association, the Joseph A. Sprague Memorial Award, an award also won by Eddie Adams), his modesty is also the key that keeps him going. "Every day I get up I have to prove myself," he admits. He loves the competition of getting to the scene first, or grabbing an exclusive, or just having better stuff than anyone else. Almost the only regret he had about leaving still photography was that he would no longer get the regular thrill of seeing his name in print. "There's still nothing like your name under the photo on page one of the paper," he said in 1992. "It's a wonderful feeling. It gives you a smile."

But the new job had plenty to offer, especially financial security. He tells a story about his first day at Channel 5, a story that helps quell any uncertainties he may have had about leaving one camera for another. There was a building collapse in Chinatown, on a rainy day. Forman was being trained in the use of the new equipment, and his supervisor had him holding an umbrella over the camera as they made their way to the scene. Forman ran into the assignment editor from the *Herald*, who joked, "So, Stanley, this is the new job." "Fifty thousand dollars a year to carry an umbrella," Forman quipped. "Any more openings?" responded the *Herald* photographer.

Forman has been a television news photographer longer than he was a still photographer, and although he has won numerous awards from the Boston Press Photographers Association for his work (five times for still photography, tying the record of his idol Rollie Oxton, and five times for videography), he talks about the difficulties of the video form. To begin with, the camera weighs twenty-two pounds, and by day's end it feels like fifty. In his early sixties, with a bad back,

Forman no longer runs to get to a story. Besides, he learned long ago that it is not always the first at the scene who gets the best shots.

It took him time to adjust to the additional demands of video. For example, now he had to think in terms not only of picture but also of sound. The job also required working more closely with reporters than he had as a still photographer. There were more scenes to think about, making sure he gave the editor enough footage to work with to tell a story. And the nature of what he had always considered news was different. For television, you could shoot a first-day story on the second or third day, catching up to what others had. With stills, either you got the news-making shot or you did not.

He also realizes that video does not have the impact of stills. To be sure, there are exceptions, such as the video of the Rodney King beating or footage from 9/11, but video is evanescent. It tends to lessen the dramatic impact, whereas stills isolate and augment it, perhaps even create it. Such is the case in comparing Joe Rosenthal's still shot with moving pictures from the flag raising at Iwo Jima. The lesson is equally clear with the assault on Landsmark. The newsreel shot by cameramen rolls by in seconds. We are shocked by the brutality of the punches and kicks, and Landsmark falling to the ground. Rakes dashes in with the flag, swings and misses, and then it is over. No isolated moment to study. No fixed image to lay claim to our souls. The video has literally faded with time. "Stills," Forman knows, "last forever."

At times, Forman has brought his still camera to the scene and joined the two sides of his photographic eye. In 1986, he came across a burning house while cruising late at night. His sequence of rescuers dropping a baby from a burning building, and other victims jumping from the roof as flames shot up into the night sky, got him the first page on many national newspapers, including the *Globe*. His award-winning video work includes a drowning in Lowell, a Goodyear blimp caught in the trees in Manchester (he was the only one to get through police lines and into the woods), and even a flag burning at the Democratic National Convention.

What Forman possesses that few photographers twenty years his junior have is an uncompromising work ethic. "Luck is the residue of hard work" is one of his favorite phrases. Clearly, preparation is a key to his success. "Some people learn a new word every day," he says. "I try to learn a new street. It's important in this job. I look at a street and think, hey, I might have to come here someday. Where is it? Is it one way? Does it dead-end? Where are the stoplights?"

Although he now has GPS, he seldom uses it. But he has scanners and pagers and radios buzzing at all times. Both his van and his house are repositories of beeping, crackling, blaring sounds. In the middle of the night his wife turns up the air-conditioning so she does not have to listen. And he turns up the volume. There's a practical side to all this: he goes out at all hours, shoots a fire or an accident or a rescue, transmits the footage from his van, goes back to bed, and earns four hours overtime. Most of the time, his wife does not even know he's gone.

As necessary as the money is, that is not what drives him. He has never lost his childhood love of the chase, of hearing sirens and standing in the swirl of action. It may be that news is now entertainment and presentation, rather than content, but Forman shuns no assignment and loves it every time his work gets on the air. That part never gets old. He continues to carry a digital still camera in each of his cars. He sometimes allows himself to dream about getting one more great shot, one more big one, not for him but for his daughters, who were born long after he first gained an international reputation for his work.

For more than forty years, Forman has worked in Boston, and he has friendships with seemingly everyone in and around town—firefighters, cops, paramedics, politicians, businessmen, journalists. In November 2006, Forman was in South Boston to cover the dedication of a playground at St. Peter Academy to Jim Kelly. Kelly spotted Forman and warmly said, "How's my friend Stan?" Politicians, students, teachers, and constituents crowded the playground for the ceremony. The mayor said, "Politics is still about people, and no one personifies the people business better than Jim Kelly." A state representative said Kelly was a fighter who "never took a step back." Suffering from cancer, Kelly managed to offer his appreciation and smiled as the children sang "God Bless America."

Kelly's visibility and relentless advocacy through the busing crisis of the 1970s brought him the devotion of South Boston residents. He was arrested numerous times for civil disobedience. Kelly was so tough that once, while he was being arrested, cops pulled at the hair on his chest and he did not flinch. He despised busing and says it was not "a black and white situation" but about fairness, and legality, and cost. Asked about Forman's photograph, he says the incident was a "mild skirmish," and it was the image that made it seem like something more. He concedes, however, that it did damage the anti-busing cause.

In the aftermath of the busing crisis, Kelly moved formally into politics and competed for City Council in 1981, running a grassroots campaign by knocking on doors and emphasizing "neighborhood stability." Though he lost narrowly, he won the support of labor unions and the police. Two years later, he was elected to the City

Council. He remained there, serving as council president from 1994 to 2000. Kelly represented District 2, which consists primarily of South Boston, the South End, and Chinatown.

Within a handful of years after his election, Kelly was at the head of another controversy over race: discrimination in public housing. The United States Department of Housing and Urban Development found that the Boston Housing Authority had discriminated against blacks in assignments to public housing projects in South Boston and ordered the wrong rectified by freezing the waiting list until minority families had received apartments. To Kelly, this smacked of unfairness, and once again his populist rhetoric came to the forefront as he talked about "forced housing" versus "freedom of choice." Accused of being racist, Kelly dismissed the charge by saying, "I am outraged by any policy that gives preference at the expense of another because of race."

Kelly's neighborhood approach may have veiled his hostility to outsiders, and the unintended consequences of his rhetoric undoubtedly perpetuated racial division and hatred. By the 1980s, however, he was not the kind of activist he had been a decade earlier. In 1988, the *Globe* described him as a "voice of restraint in a segment of the community that is again rattling sabers, feeling betrayed and singled out for social experimentation." Kelly would work for what he believed in through the courts, through politics, and through reasoned debate that took place, preferably, away from the media. "I will not pander to the press," he said repeatedly. When the first black families moved into South Boston's McCormack housing project, Kelly stayed away. "I don't go and introduce myself and welcome every white family that moves in either," he said. But he also "took it as a personal responsibility," he promised, "to make sure that no black families felt threatened and that no South Boston kids were arrested for civil rights violations."

In the 1990s, Kelly opposed any affirmative action plans for hiring. Again, he expressed his central concern in terms of fairness, the major chord of his political philosophy. In a forum on race with President Bill Clinton, Kelly said he understood that one of the legacies of slavery was black poverty, but there were many poor whites as well, and the only question that mattered was whether they were "fit and willing and qualified." Kelly called for hearings at the City Council and said, "There is a lot of unfair treatment to people who take the test [for city employment], pass it, but because of their race they are being denied the opportunity." In a liberal city, Kelly was accused of divisiveness, but his conservative position (he described himself as "a union-oriented Reagan Democrat") was fueled less by racism than by the only desire that governed his political career: supporting the sanctity of neighborhoods and the needs of his constituents. To anyone listening carefully, Kelly said as much when, in talking about majority-black districts, he acknowledged that "if I was the district councilor from Mattapan, I'd probably agree that racial set-asides are a necessity." One supporter from the South End said, "He's constituent-oriented. He doesn't care what the color of your skin is, what your personal beliefs are, what nationality you belong to."

Though one might not glean it from his positions on housing discrimination and affirmative action, Kelly's racial attitudes had changed. If in the seventies he was heard to yell racial epithets, he now defended equal rights and treatment. He helped work on a human rights ordinance and made it clear, according to one councilor, "that he is opposed to any people being victims of violence or discrimination." At the same time, he supported everyone's right to associate with whomever they pleased. Asked about racism in 1988, he told the *Herald*, "If you define racism as someone who willfully denies people of the opposite race their rights, someone with a hatred of other races, no I'm not . . . It suits the liberals' purposes," he argued, "to paint everyone who opposed forced busing as a racist." In 1994, Kelly said, "I don't think someone is a racist simply because they're more comfortable with associating with their own people with whom they have much in common . . . Do I want to see blacks get good decent jobs and to live in good, safe neighborhoods and go to school and get a good education? I want all those things for blacks, Hispanics, Asians as much as I want them for people in my own neighborhood." But that did not mean he wanted his daughter to marry a black man or a foreigner, he said. If Kelly's honesty made the liberals squirm, so be it.

For Kelly, the neighborhood was everything. Much of his social and political philosophy through the 1980s and '90s was governed by an almost nostalgic desire to preserve a South Boston that, in reality, no longer existed. "I just don't see why the neighborhood has to change," he lamented in 1993. "I don't see why it has to be any different than when I was growing up there." But even as he spoke, South Boston, like the city at large, was being transformed. A study conducted in 1999 found that 37 percent of South Boston residents entered the city after 1990, and a total of 48 percent of the people in the community were not born or raised there. The central reference point of Kelly's career, the busing crisis of the 1970s, had no meaning to these newcomers.

Described time and again as the council's "hardest-working member" and as someone who consistently delivered services to his constituents, Kelly relentlessly (some might say ruthlessly) defended his district. He battled with the mayor and the Boston Redevelopment Authority over development of the seaport, wanting the area to be known as the South Boston Seaport, opposing the building of new housing that would gentrify the area, and creating the controversial South Boston Betterment Trust, which negotiated and received payments from developers for commercial projects.

Kelly's district is currently about 66 percent white, 8 percent black, 10 percent Hispanic, and 15 percent Asian. A devout Irish Catholic, he remained a steadfast social conservative (he opposed the Supreme Judicial Court's ruling allowing for gay marriage in Massachusetts). But he worked tirelessly for his constituents, regardless of their race, occupation, or ideology. Ill with cancer, Kelly still made time every week to respond to the voters. His beloved South Boston was not his childhood neighborhood any longer, but he steadfastly fought for it until he passed away at age sixty-six on January 9, 2007. One African American politician summed up his years of service this way: "regardless of how you might feel about his stands, he's absolutely been an institution and a beloved public servant to the people of South Boston."

In the late 1980s, Landsmark bumped into Kelly around City Hall. He had heard that Kelly was in Forman's photograph, and he asked him about it. Kelly smiled enigmatically and didn't answer. But in the years after that he always called Landsmark "Teddy" and treated him as one of the inner circle.

Ted Landsmark had also found his way into politics, though he never ran for elective office. In 1988, Mayor Ray Flynn appointed Landsmark director of the Mayor's Office of Jobs and Community Services and, a year or two later, director of the Safe Neighborhoods Project. Since his election as mayor in 1984, Flynn had worked to heal the racial fissures opened by the busing crisis. Appointing prominent black and Latino leaders to positions in city government was one of his ways of reaching out. Landsmark's office was responsible for fighting poverty and providing job training. His work as a dean had been satisfying, and Landsmark did much to promote multicultural education and affirmative action policies. But Landsmark decided to join Flynn after listening in horror as his former boss Michael Dukakis mishandled a question on rape in a presidential debate, an issue with racial overtones because the Republicans had politicized Dukakis's decision as governor to furlough a black inmate who had been convicted of sexual assault. Landsmark felt a responsibility "to get my hands dirty again" and to get involved in "the public sector where my day-to-day actions will have an immediate impact."

Landsmark did an outstanding job in the mayor's office. He helped organize forums, provided youths with summer jobs, created local networks, and coordinated community-based health activities. His understanding of the importance of community action and involvement was central to his success. One could not simply wait for the police to stop crime; with his leadership, activists and parents worked with police authorities to fight it. He also provided grants to other groups, such as Gang Peace, which sought to help youths turn negative relationships into positive ones. The efforts contributed to a dramatic decline in the homicide rate in Boston, by 25 percent citywide and 53 percent in Roxbury, Dorchester, and Mattapan.

Mayor Flynn also took quick action to try to curtail racial violence. When a black South Boston public housing resident was beaten with a baseball bat, Flynn revived a Civil Rights Cabinet and placed Landsmark in charge. The group, consisting of high officials from various city agencies and departments, met monthly and sought to mobilize, in Landsmark's words, "a broad spectrum of community support for the basic human and civil rights of all our citizens." Landsmark also organized interdenominational services of peace and healing in South Boston and Charlestown.

The most inflammatory racial event since busing to erupt in Boston occurred in October 1989 when Charles Stuart reported that his pregnant wife was killed and he was shot in the stomach by a black assailant in the Mission Hill district, an integrated neighborhood. Police aggressively pursued various suspects and made an arrest. But Stuart's brother told police that it was Charles who killed his wife and wounded himself. The case ended on January 4, 1990, when Stuart committed suicide. The racial reverberations would have lasted longer but for Flynn's understanding that his office had to respond forcefully to the racial profiling that had taken place. He had Landsmark study the way the media overplayed the racial aspects of the case and cast Mission Hill in an unfavorable light. Flynn sought a rational and coordinated approach to the portrayal of the city and addressed specific substantive neighborhood needs such as economic development and youth services. In the end, says Landsmark, "a deranged and suicidal individual was using race for his own selfish purposes." With his advice, Flynn was able to defuse the situation, ease tensions in Mission Hill, and explain how "it turned out we were all victims of a sinister hoax."

Landsmark's only misstep, it seems, came the first time he addressed an issue directly related to public education. Comments he made off the record in 1993 about METCO, the voluntary busing program started in 1966 that sent inner-city children to suburban schools, drew him close to the third rail of Boston politics. Landsmark suggested phasing out METCO so that the Boston public schools could reap the benefit of the thirty-five hundred students not in the system. "We cannot hope to improve the quality of our neighborhood schools," Landsmark said, "without the participation of active parents whose upwardly mobile aspirations for their children are an essential ingredient in an improved learning environment." METCO supporters denounced Landsmark and proclaimed that his comments were an insult to the students and parents in Boston's public schools. They called him "a lazy bureaucrat" and accused him of looking for "scapegoats." Landsmark was not politically naive, but still the reaction took him by surprise. Even the black community ostracized him. He merely thought that the energy and ambition of those parents whose students travel to the suburbs every day would have an impact if employed in neighborhood public schools. He recalled that he too had been bused, but one of the consequences was feeling detached from where he lived as well as where he went to school. The controversy passed, and it would be a while before Landsmark would again comment on Boston's public schools.

The following year, when he was working as an aide to newly elected Mayor Thomas Menino, Landsmark looked up as his office door opened. In wandered a man filled with sorrow and in search of forgiveness. Bobby Powers, one of Landsmark's attackers nearly twenty years earlier, introduced himself. "It is with great humility that I approach you and tell you that I was the individual who initiated the attack on you," Powers said. Landsmark heard Powers's confession, and the two talked for an hour. Powers told a *Boston Herald* reporter, "I always blamed busing for a lot of my problems. But a lot of my problems were with myself." After 1976, Powers faced various legal problems and fell into alcoholism. He realized he could never move forward without confronting what he had done.

"I was not a racist," Powers said. "I was just an angry young man, a boy really . . . I wanted to make amends, I'm not a hateful person." Powers now had a son, and he wanted desperately to break the cycle of hatred that twisted his life. So Powers asked Landsmark for forgiveness, but Ted told him he had forgiven his attackers long ago. Indeed, he said, "I always identified with the young men who attacked me. I've never forgotten that I grew up in public housing projects in East Harlem." He added, "I've gotten beyond that experience. It happened so long ago that it feels like it happened to a different person."

By 1997, Landsmark had left the mayor's office to become president of the Boston Architectural Center, where he has remained since then. Now the Boston Architectural College, the BAC offers degrees in architecture, landscape, and design. Founded as a club for architects in 1889, the BAC has emerged as a central institution for degree programs, continuing education, and professional development in the field of architecture and design. Becoming president of the BAC fulfilled for Landsmark a lifelong quest: "I first dreamed of being an architect when I was a small black kid growing up with my mother in Harlem's public housing projects." Landsmark had shied away from becoming a practicing architect because of the isolation that he feared would engulf him as a black man in an overwhelmingly white profession. Now, as president, he could not only pursue his interest in shaping the built environment but also work on the issue of diversity in what he called "the most recalcitrant of professions."

In 2002, Landsmark became chair of the American Institute of Architects Diversity Committee. He has insisted on better demographic analysis so the profession can track exactly who its members are, helped create mentoring and internship programs, investigated shorter routes to liscensure, and called for transformation in the studio culture of a profession that can be extremely difficult on women and minorities. Bringing together thirty years of experience as a lawyer, policymaker, civil rights activist, and educator, Landsmark has cogently made the case for why difference matters: "We must recognize that diversity and inclusiveness bring out not only different people, but different ways of thinking. Instead of feeling threatened by ideas that don't simply reflect the thoughts and ideas we already have, we should celebrate our differences, and learn to love the richness that diversity brings. We are better design professionals and better citizens when we open our minds and hearts to different ways of thinking."

At the time Landsmark became president of BAC, he was also engaged in graduate studies to deepen his understanding of African American culture. In 1999, he received a doctoral degree in American Studies from Boston University for his study of nineteenth-century African American crafts. Landsmark examined the work of black artisans, both slave and free, and discussed the challenges of collecting, exhibiting, and interpreting vernacular crafts. In a lecture on "Race and Place," delivered at the Boston Athenaeum in 2004, Landsmark drew on his expertise to discuss the markers of identity in American culture. He talked about the civic life of the city and displayed cultural artifacts from the past—including a wood plane made by a black artisan—as a point of entry for engaging those whose experiences are different. "We are living in a new city," he declared, a city in which being black meant you were as likely to be African as American, from Senegal or Nigeria as from South Carolina or Georgia. The new racial and ethnic diversity of Boston, he continued, meant finding ways to bring those who were part of a "marginalized social class" into full participation in Boston.

Landsmark also used the occasion to discuss a task force he was chairing at the request of the mayor. Its mandate was to gather public input on creating a new system for student assignment to Boston's public schools. For all the work that Landsmark had done under two mayors, he had never before been directly involved in educational policy. But, in another sense, since everyone knew him as the man at the center of Forman's photograph, he was seen as having always been at the center of the battle over busing. In choosing Landsmark, Menino sent a signal that whatever new policies emerged, they would not mark a return to the racial divisiveness of the 1970s.

In accepting the position, Landsmark noted that "life is full of ironic opportunities." The risk of chairing the task force meant inviting countless questions about the photograph, something Landsmark preferred not to talk about. "My life has been a lot more interesting than the twenty-second moment captured in that picture," he says. For years he did not own a copy of the picture, but he recently acquired a print, framed it, and placed it on the wall by his desk. An avid collector of art, he has in his office another recent purchase: the 1856 lithograph that depicts Crispus Attucks at the center of the Boston Massacre.

In taking on leadership of the task force, Landsmark was doing what he had done for nearly thirty years, serving the city he cherishes and helping find ways for it to move to a brighter future. If that also meant transcending in the public eye his place in Forman's photograph, so much the better.

The school assignment system that Landsmark and his colleagues investigated no longer included race as a factor. In 1999, twenty-five years after the court decision that compelled Boston to desegregate its schools, the Boston School Committee, no longer elected but now appointed by the mayor, voted 5–2 to drop race in placing students. Facing a lawsuit that argued the system discriminated against whites, and reading a national legal landscape in which the courts were overturning affirmative action plans, Boston chose to seek other ways to balance school choice and class diversity. Besides, the demographics of the city had changed dramatically, with public school enrollment 49 percent black, 26 percent Hispanic, 15 percent white, and 9 percent Asian. The controlled choice system adopted in 1989, in which the city was divided into three zones and a variety of factors—proximity, race, lottery, family preference— determined what school a student attended, would continue, but with racial preference eliminated.

Skeptics saw Landsmark as providing political cover for a mayor who had already decided that busing was costing the city too much (some fifty-nine million dollars a year) and that a return to neighborhood schools might work. But Landsmark was no one's shill, and he approached a series of open town meetings across the city with the goal of understanding what it was that parents wanted for their children's education. He discovered a complexity that belied stereotype: "We've heard from some African-American and Latino parents in Roxbury who would like to have their children attend schools closer to home, and we've heard from some white parents in West Roxbury who would like the system to maintain some form of choice." Preconceptions would have predicted the reverse.

Landsmark found that the policymakers had never really sought to understand what the parents wanted out of their schools. Above all else, parents wanted excellence. They desired a quality education for their children, and they demanded access. They wanted openness in decision-making, and they especially wanted to be treated with respect by school authorities. They desired diversity, but they wanted it along with high expectations for educational achievement. Most striking of all, he found that the issue that seemed most salient for the politicians meant next to nothing to their constituents: the past.

The demographic reality of Boston in 2004 was that it was peopled by residents who had not lived in Boston in the 1970s—indeed, who had not been born until after the crisis of busing had subsided. According to one estimate, some 80 percent of Boston's black population did not reside in Boston at the time of the busing crisis. "The number of people who carry the baggage of Boston's racism is very few," observes Landsmark. That was not to say that they had not experienced their own incidents of racial prejudice and ostracism. But it meant that they were not burdened by the weight of having experienced the busing crisis firsthand. "You might as well be talking to them about Lincoln freeing the slaves," Landsmark emphasizes, "as talk to them about busing and how it tore neighborhoods apart."

It is a striking observation, and it gets to the essence of one of the ways reputations change: the passage of time. A writer once commented that "history democratizes our sensibilities." He meant that as time goes by we forget the details, we lose our sense of absolute right and wrong, we forgive the dead. And while those who battled against one another in the 1970s over the issue of busing are not about to join together on a nostalgic walk across City Hall Plaza, the survivors—most of them, anyhow—have obtained some peace. For everyone else, it is a history with which they are not personally saddled.

If the crisis of busing has slipped into long-ago history, it has also been submerged by a reversal in attitudes toward desegregation. As many educators have shown, most notably Gary Orfield and his associates at the Civil Rights Project, the more than fifty years since *Brown v. Board of Education* have not been kind to the dream of integration. Indeed, there has been a massive resegregation of the schools throughout the nation over the past quarter century. This has occurred despite Orfield's finding that "Americans of all races express a preference for integrated education and believe it is very important for their children to learn to understand and work with others of different racial and ethnic backgrounds."

As a result of the actions of a conservative Supreme Court that has reversed itself on questions of desegregation and affirmative action programs, a failure of political leadership, profound demographic shifts in the makeup of cities, and the eventual loss of a social sense of urgency once de jure segregation had been eliminated, school resegregation and educational inequality have soared. Jonathan Kozol, who has devoted his career to promoting good learning in urban public schools, calls the problem "America's educational apartheid," a system where no one any longer speaks of racial segregation and instead uses "linguistic sweeteners, semantic somersaults, and surrogate vocabularies to talk around the problem." Fifty years after *Brown*, still separate and still unequal is Kozol's judgment on America's schools.

That is not to say the 1954 decision was a failure. Legal, publicly funded discrimination had been eliminated. And some urban school districts have managed, despite the retreat from integration, to show impressive gains in student achievement, none more so than Boston's, which in 2006 won the half-million-dollar Broad Prize for demonstrating "the greatest overall performance and improvement in student achievement while reducing achievement gaps for poor and minority students." The struggle against segregation and racism, like the struggle for quality education, requires constant vigilance and generations of community leaders willing to reinvest old ideals with new currency.

Such is the case in Boston. If the city today is more cosmopolitan, sophisticated, diverse, and tolerant than it was three decades ago, it is that way because of the concerted effort of people like Landsmark. He had every reason to flee in 1976, and every reason to be angry and unforgiving, but instead he stayed and served with distinction. Asked if he thinks Boston is a racist city, he immediately answers no. The racial climate "is a completely different world" than it was in the 1970s. "The city has matured," he says. "It is more accepting of difference." To be sure, there has not yet been a black mayor (unlike in New York, Philadelphia, and Atlanta), and that would certainly help boost its reputation, but the city is no more racist than any other. Stanley Forman agrees: "I can't believe it's a racist city. I can't believe it's any different than any other city." He says that Boston has succeeded in recent years in altering its image, an image fixed by his photograph.

In 2002, *Boston* magazine asked, "Is Boston Racist?" and found that while there was still significant residential segregation, Boston's self-image was out of step with how the rest of the nation viewed the city. The magazine polled people living elsewhere and found that they overwhelmingly thought of the place as progressive. To change Boston's reputation from within, a new generation of leaders have worked together to transform the feel and character of the city. They have increased minority voting, forged partnerships with businesses and cultural institutions, and created support networks for black professionals. Equally important, blacks in Boston have decided no longer to remain invisible in the civic and cultural life of the city.

That does not mean Forman's photograph has vanished. Nearly every comment about the city's progress mentions the picture. It is the reference point against which all change is measured. *Boston* magazine reminded readers that "because the busing era became so entrenched in people's minds thanks to a photo of a white man attacking a black man with the pole of a big American flag, that past still clings to the city." The photograph cannot be erased. But it can be engaged, and its meaning can be transformed.

The Soiling of Old Glory captures an instant of unthinkable racial hatred. The photograph would lead, at first, to turmoil and self-scrutiny, and later, to progress and healing. Some may have remained forever chilled by being caught in that frozen moment. But others could gaze beyond the frame. They had personal and professional work to do, work on behalf of a broken city that they loved.

AFTERWORD

A VOICE ON the phone said, "This is Joseph Rakes." I was in the gym, expecting my daughter to call for a ride home from school. Though I knew parts of Rakes's story, it troubled me that I had not spoken to the man wielding the flag in the photograph. I had talked to Forman, Landsmark, and Kelly. I needed to talk to Rakes, or at least try. I wrote him a letter explaining my project, expressing respect for his privacy, and saying I hoped that he would contact me. A few days later, my cell phone rang while I was exercising. Surprised and breathless, I made certain to schedule time the next day to speak with him.

I spent an uneasy evening imagining possible scenarios and trying to contrive ways to ask necessary questions politely. As is usually the case, the conversation went differently than I imagined. I thought Rakes might be curt and defensive, offering brief responses. After all, he had spoken at length to only one reporter in the more than thirty years since the incident. But Rakes was open and talkative.

The assault on the morning of April 5 was "all a blur," he said, and had been from the moment it happened. He described the "blind rage" of the event, an outpouring of anger and resentment that had accrued since September 1974 when he was set to enter tenth grade at South Boston High School.

Rakes had loved school. His father had always told him and his siblings that they each had a job to do: his was to go to work; theirs was to go to school. He recalls having missed only a few days in ninth grade, due to the flu. But suddenly it all changed. That first day in September 1974 he showed up with new shoes, ready to start, but there would be no going to school that day, or many days after that for the entire year.

The situation worsened. He described a community that was "depressed and mad." And the students each day had to prepare for battle, not against blacks, he emphasized, but against the police. For him and his friends, the situation "wasn't so much black and white as blue." The tactical police force regularly harassed the teens, who could not walk in groups of more than three without being stopped and accused of violating laws prohibiting crowds on the streets. "If you came home and you weren't bleeding, you were okay," he recalls.

The days inside South Boston High pulsated with tension. Every time there was an incident, Rakes says, the police would lock down the building and drive their riot sticks through the classroom door handles, keeping everyone in their rooms. "Everyone was a victim. Everyone got dragged into it," he says.

What few recreational outlets he enjoyed were closed. Rakes had been a competitive swimmer, but the racial tensions put an end to various sports programs, and he decided he simply did not want to participate in what was available.

The anger that built up in school and on the streets did not abate at home. Rakes's father, like so many South Boston parents, opposed busing. His father had started as a janitor at Gillette and worked his way up to be head of maintenance, with thirty men under him. And still, on his last day of work before he retired, he grabbed the brush and scrubbed the toilets. Whereas Rakes's mother was "100 percent Irish," his father was Greek, almost Cuban looking. He remembers them as appearing like Lucy and Ricky from the *I Love Lucy* television comedy. But his father was no South Boston outsider. He loved the community and could not understand "how you tell someone to get on a bus two hours earlier when you can see the school outside your window."

In 1975–76, Rakes quit school altogether. He took a job to help pay the family bills that now carried the added expense (six hundred dollars per year) of sending his older siblings to the South Boston Heights Academy, created as an alternative private school for those opting out of the public system. Rakes too would attend the Heights Academy, where he resumed playing sports. He recalls getting donated shirts from a union club for team uniforms. The shirts read PICK AND SHOVEL CLUB, but at least the participants looked respectable and organized. He graduated in 1977.

By then, he had been convicted of assaulting Ted Landsmark and given a two-year suspended sentence and two years' probation. At the time of the attack on April 5, Rakes thought little of the incident. He was angry and waved his flag in the direction of a black man, who was taking a beating from others. He didn't know whether he had connected or not. It passed so quickly, and then it was over.

The next afternoon he was riding the train to his part-time job cleaning offices downtown. He looked across the aisle and saw Forman's photograph on the front page of the *Herald American*. Within days, everyone knew it was Rakes wielding the flag in a photograph that horrified the nation. He hated being identified as the "flag kid," and in the patriotic precincts of South Boston few thought him a hero. He had made the community look bad, a community that he cherished. His girlfriend broke up with him, but he would suffer harsher punishments.

After graduating, Rakes, with the help of his retired father, took a job as a janitor at Gillette. His supervisor, a black woman, recognized him as the student with the flag from City Hall Plaza. A day later, he was jumped in the men's room by two or three black guys, payback for the attack on Landsmark. He had been in plenty of fights before, and he knows that the experience "makes you hard." He means it both ways—toughens you up and forms a shell.

He quit, knowing that he would probably have to fight his way through work every day. Instead, he found jobs that were more solitary: he was a lifeguard at a boys' club, drove a taxi, and eventually started working construction. He felt more comfortable being isolated and alone. He could just do his work, earn his living, and not have to worry about involvement with others.

Once he returned to Boston in 1988, after fleeing charges in the assault on his sister's boyfriend, Rakes started to settle down. The key for him was reconnecting with the girl of his dreams, who suddenly found herself widowed with three children. Rakes had known her since they were little. He says she was his fantasy date to a prom, but back then she was "untouchable" to a guy like him. They married in 1996, and together they have had children of their own.

Rakes and his wife scraped together enough money to buy a house some one hundred miles north of Boston. From there, Rakes commuted to a construction job on the central artery. He says he is not afraid of hard work, and over time he moved up the ladder in the union hall. His grandmother once advised him to "find a job no one wants to do and get good at it." Rakes specializes in hazardous waste.

I ask Rakes about the effect of the photograph on his life. He pauses. Without it "life might have gone a different way," he says. What dismayed him was learning years later that, though he had been convicted of hitting Landsmark with the flag, he had not actually landed a blow. He wonders whether, had that been made clear at the time, he would not have been convicted of assault with a dangerous weapon. Maybe without a criminal record, he might have had a shot at a different career. But missed opportunities are part of life, he adds. The incident was a long time ago, and he is long over it, refusing to dwell on what might have been had he stayed out of the attack, or had that picture never been made. The photograph captures the rage of a teenager forced to grow up too fast. He was only seventeen, and he feels he should have been "allowed to fuck up." But he is not that person anymore. "Life goes on," he says.

In 2001, before the *Boston Globe* reported on the twenty-fifth anniversary of the photograph, Rakes called together a group of black construction workers who labored with him on the Big Dig. Eight men gathered in a room, and Rakes told them about the picture. He said it would soon appear in the newspaper, and he did not want them surprised by the article. He asked if anyone had a problem with him because of it. Only a single person on the crew knew anything about the photograph. Another crew member thought he might have some trouble working with someone who had committed a racial assault, but he appreciated that Rakes understood why. An older Jamaican seemed to speak for all when he said, "Shit happens." An uneasy silence filled the room. These men felt more comfortable with tools than with words. After a few moments, they shuffled outside and went back to work, clearing a tunnel of debris.

ACKNOWLEDGMENTS

MY GREATEST DEBT is to Stanley Forman, whose enthusiastic response to my initial query several years ago made this book possible. He has had a remarkable career, and I am grateful to him for sharing his stories as well as his pictures. I am also deeply grateful to Theodore Landsmark, Joseph Rakes, and the late James Kelly for talking about the incident, the photograph, and their experiences. William Bulger kindly discussed the busing crisis with me over a memorable breakfast at Mul's Diner in South Boston. Bob Allison not only introduced me to key people and relevant documents, he has also been a steadfast friend for nearly twenty years.

I received indispensable assistance from numerous archivists and librarians. My thanks to John Dorsey (Boston Public Library), Marisa Hudspeth (Northeastern University Special Collections and Archives), Keith Luf (WGBH Archives), Yvette Reyes (AP), Kristen Swett (City of Boston Archives), and Donna Wells (Boston Police Department). I am also indebted to the many specialists at the following institutions and organizations who granted permission to reproduce the images in this book: American Antiquarian Society, Art & Commerce, Associated Press Photos, Black Star, Duke University Special Collections, Library of Congress, Magnum, Museum of Modern Art, Northeastern University Archives, Pace/MacGill Gallery, the Robert Mapplethorpe Foundation, and Viamse Musea. Thanks as well to Lisa Bitel, Jerry Hirniak, Monica Karales, Faith Ringgold, Dread Scott, and Richard Skolnik. Photographers are among the most generous professionals I have ever met: I owe a special debt of gratitude to Tom Franklin of the *Bergen Record*.

Over the years, I was fortunate to have three first-rate research assistants: Carol Quirke, Barrett Wilson-Murphy, and Thomas Roland Brown. It was also my great good luck to take a position at Trinity College in September 2004. I offer my thanks to President James Jones, interim dean Frank Kirkpatrick, and Dean Rena Fraden. My colleagues in the American Studies program have been remarkably supportive. I am grateful to Eugene Leach, Margo Perkins, Scott Tang, Cheryl Greenberg, Joan Hedrick, Barbara Sicherman, Rob Corber, and Andrew Walsh. I should also like to thank Zayde Antrim, Jeff Bayliss, Jen Bowman, Ned Cabot, Jack Chatfield, Sean Cocco, Pablo Delano, Jack Dougherty, Jonathan Elukin, Dario Euraque, Luis Figueroa, Renny Fulco, Stephanie Gilmore, Rick Hazleton, Dan Heischman, Sam Kassow, Kathleen Kete, Paul Lauter, Michael Lestz, Kevin McMahon, Susan Pennybacker, Gary Reger, Robin Sheppard, Mark Silk, and Ron Spencer. Without Gigi St. Peter and Nancy Rossi, administrative assistants for History and American Studies respectively, I would have lost my way long ago. The students in the American Studies Program at Trinity have provided a constant source of energy and excitement. I am grateful as well to Coach Bill Decker and the Trinity College baseball team.

My friends in Highland Park have come through time and again. I am indebted to them for many kindnesses, whether lunch at the Dish, backyard barbecues, or the occasional Friday night poker game. My gratitude to Jeff and Audrey Roderman, Bart Moore and Debra Osinsky, Peter Guarnaccia and Linda Melamed, Saul Salkin and Maryann Thein, Allan and Marianne Feinberg, and Darren Staloff.

Several friends read either part or all of the manuscript, and their comments helped make this a better book. I offer my deepest thanks to Bob Allison, Kathy Feeley, Scott Gac, Jim Goodman, Doug Greenberg, and Tom Slaughter for taking time out of their busy schedules. I am especially grateful to Aaron Sachs, who has been teaching me how to write since he was an undergraduate and I was his adviser, and to Peter Mancall, for his unconditional support and good humor. As always, Dave Masur, Bruce Rossky, and Mark Richman have known precisely when to ask about my writing and, more important, when not to. It has been a rewarding experience to work with Peter Ginna, and I am pleased to be among the first authors he has published at Bloomsbury Press. Katie Henderson kept everything on track and responded to my queries instantaneously. I am delighted to have been reunited with publicist Peter Miller. I greatly appreciate the efforts of Zoe Pagnamenta, who has believed in this project from the start.

I met Tom Slaughter, Doug Greenberg, and Jim Goodman in graduate school, Tom and Doug my first semester, Jim a few years later. I have a photograph of us, outside a pizza joint in Princeton, with Denise, Margee, and Jenny, and Molly, Ben, and Sam (Gracie, Sophie, Jackson, Moses, and Jasmine born later). There are many other photographs over the decades. But I especially enjoy gazing at this one. I look and I think how blessed I am to have had such giving, loving friends for all of these years, friends with whom I have shared great times and hard, and who continue to inspire me.

In March 2006, I delivered an inaugural lecture for the Kenan Professorship. In a packed auditorium, in the middle of my talk, I caught the eyes of my wife, Jani, and our children, Ben and Sophie. That instant was the happiest moment of my career, the point where the professional and the personal came together. So what if their eyes were a bit glazed over? The songwriter from New Jersey sings "what else can we do now / Except roll down the window / And let the wind blow back your hair." The road stretches before us, and our love remains forever wild, forever real.

BIBLIOGRAPHIC ESSAY

MY ACCOUNT OF the incident in chapter 1 is based on conversations with Stanley Forman, Ted Landsmark, Jim Kelly, and Joseph Rakes as well as the reports published at the time in the *Boston Globe*, *Boston Herald American*, and *Boston Phoenix*. In addition, I have examined the newsreel footage of the assault as well as reports of the incident that aired on The Ten O'Clock News in Boston and ABC News nationally.

On Landsmark, see Thomas Farragher, "Image of an Era," *Boston Globe*, April 1, 2001; "Profile: Ted Landsmark: The Unsung of Civil Rights," *Morning Edition,* National Public Radio, February 1, 2000; John Koch, "Ted Landsmark: The Interview," *Boston Globe Magazine*, March 7, 1999; Edward Zuckerman, "Beaten Up in Boston," *New Republic*, May 22, 1976, 9–12; Brenda Payton, " 'I Was Just a Nigger They Were Trying to Kill,' " *Boston Phoenix*, April 13, 1976, 16. On Forman, see Ron Winslow, "The Big One," *Boston Magazine*, June 1981, 114–19; 155–60; Michael Delaney and James Gordon, "Boston's Stan the Man," *News Photographer*, April 1979, 12–17; Karen Rothmyer, "Stanley Forman: Capturing Drama Through the Photographer's Lens," in *Winning Pulitzers: 76 Stories Behind Some of the Best News Coverage of Our Time* (1991); Yana Dlugy, "Shifting Gears:

From Newspaper to Television," *News Photographer*, July 1992, 13–17; Stanley Forman, "A Night's Work," *News Photographer*, January 1987, 50–52; Stanley Forman, "The Best Picture I Never Took," *Nieman Foundation for Journalism at Harvard University* 52 (Summer 1998); Stanley Forman, "Chasing the Big One," unpublished manuscript; *Moment of Impact: Stories of the Pulitzer Prize Photographs* (Haber Video, 1999). On Kelly, see Suzanne Perney, "Will the Real Jim Kelly Please Stand Up?" *Boston Sunday Herald*, December 4, 1988. Also see the brief account of the incident in J. Anthony Lukas, *Common Ground: A Turbulent Decade in the Lives of Three American Families* (1985), 323–26, and Celia Wren, "Stars and Strife," *Smithsonian*, April 2006, 21–22.

The story of Boston and busing, synthesized in chapter 2, has been the subject of numerous books. The best overarching portrait is provided by J. Anthony Lukas, *Common Ground*. For a superb study of anti-busing, see Ronald P. Formisano, *Boston Against Busing: Race, Class, and Ethnicity in the 1960s and 1970s* (1991). Also useful is J. Michael Ross and William M. Berg, *"I Respectfully Diasagree with the Judge's Order": The Boston School Desegregation Controversy* (1981); Frank Levy, *Northern Schools and Civil Rights: The Racial Imbalance Act of Massachusetts* (1971); Alan Lupo, *Liberty's Chosen Home: The Politics of Violence in Boston* (1977); George R. Metcalf, *From Little Rock to Boston: The History of School Desegregation* (1983); J. Brian Sheehan, *The Boston School Integration Dispute: Social Change and Legal Maneuvers* (1984); Jack Tager, *Boston Riots: Three Centuries of Social Violence* (2001); D. Garth Taylor, *Public Opinion and Collective Action: The Boston School Desegregation Conflict* (1986); Jeanne F. Theoharis, " 'We Saved the City': Black Struggles for Educational Equality in Boston, 1960–1976," *Radical History Review* 81 (Fall 2001): 61–93. Also see

Susan E. Eaton, *The Other Boston Busing Story: What's Won and Lost Across the Boundary Line* (2001). For accounts and reflections by participants, see Ione Malloy, *Southie Won't Go: A Teacher's Diary of the Desegregation of South Boston High School* (1986); William M. Bulger, *While the Music Lasts: My Life in Politics* (1996); Mel King, *Chain of Change: Struggles for Black Community Development* (1981); Michael Patrick MacDonald, *All Souls: A Family Story from Southie* (1999). Also see Judith F. Buncher, ed., *The School Busing Controversy, 1970–75* (1975), and the two-reel microfilm clipping file on busing located at the Boston Public Library (microfilm/LC214.53.B67B38X).

On the history of Boston, see Robert J. Allison, *A Short History of Boston* (2004); Stephen Kendrick and Paul Kendrick, *Sarah's Long Walk: The Free Blacks of Boston and How Their Struggle for Equality Changed America* (2004); James Oliver Horton and Lois E. Horton, *Black Bostonians: Family Life and Community Struggle in the Antebellum North* (1979); Thomas H. O'Connor, *South Boston, My Home Town: The History of an Ethnic Neighborhood* (1988; new ed. 1994); Mark R. Schneider, *Boston Confronts Jim Crow, 1890–1920* (1997) and "The Boston NAACP and the Decline of the Abolitionist Impulse," *Massachusetts Historical Review* 1 (1999), www.historycooperative.org/journals/mhr/1/schneider.html; Glenn Stout and Richard Johnson, *Red Sox Century* (2000; rev. ed. 2005). A superb study of northern segregation is Davison M. Douglas, *Jim Crow Moves North: The Battle over Northern School Segregation, 1865–1954* (2005). On the Supreme Court, see Michael J. Klarman, *From Jim Crow to Civil Rights: The Supreme Court and the Struggle for Racial Equality* (2004); James T. Patterson, *Brown v. Board of Education: A Civil Rights Milestone and Its Troubled Legacy* (2001); Bernard Schwartz, *Swann's Way: The School Busing Case and the Supreme Court* (1986).

There is a vast literature on the history and theory of photography, which informs chapter 3. Essential works include John Berger, *Ways of Seeing* (1972); Henri Cartier-Bresson, *The Mind's Eye: Writings on Photography and Photographers* (1999); Geoff Dyer, *The Ongoing Moment* (2005); Vicki Goldberg, *The Power of Photography: How Photographs Changed Our Lives* (1991); Vicki Goldberg and Robert Silberman, *American Photography: A Century of Images* (1999); James Guimond, *American Photography and the American Dream* (1991); Beaumont Newhall, ed., *Photography: Essays and Images* (1980); Susan Sontag, *On Photography* (1977) and *Regarding the Pain of Others* (2003); William Stott, *Documentary Expression and Thirties America* (1973); John Szarkowski, *Looking at Photographs* (1973); Alan Trachtenberg, *Reading American Photographs: Images as History, Mathew Brady to Walker Evans* (1989). Most of the work focuses on documentary photographers and photojournalists. There is all too little writing on spot news photographers, and what there is examines combat photographers. See, for example, Susan D. Moeller, *Shooting War: Photography and the American Experience of Combat* (1989). Arthur Fellig (Weegee) is one of the few news photographers whose work is considered alongside the great documentary photographers. See *Weegee's New York: Photographs 1935–1960* (2006) and *Naked City* (1945; rpt. 2002).

On Joe Rosenthal's photograph, see Karal Ann Marling and John Wetenhall, *Iwo Jima: Monuments, Memories, and the American Hero* (1991); Parker Bishop Albee Jr. and Keller Cushing Freeman, *Shadow of Suribachi: Raising the Flags on Iwo Jima* (1995); James Bradley and Ron Powers, *Flags of Our Fathers* (2000); Hal Buell, *Uncommon Valor, Common Virtue: Iwo Jima and the Photograph That Captured America* (2006). On Paul Revere and the Boston Massacre, see Clarence Brigham, *Paul Revere's Engravings* (rev. ed. 1969); Hiller B. Zobel, *The Boston Massacre* (1970); Robert J. Allison, *The Boston Massacre* (2006). Studies of the iconography of crucifixion include Vladimir Gurewich, "Observations on the Iconography of the Wound in Christ's Side, with Special Reference to Its Position," *Journal of the Warburg and Courtauld Institutes* 20 (1957): 358–62. In *Everything That Rises: A Book of Convergences* (2006), Lawrence Weschler examines visual echoes and connections.

The history of Old Glory, narrated in chapter 4, is addressed in Marc Leepson, *Flag: An American Biography* (2005); Robert E. Bonner, "Star-Spangled Sentiment," *Common-place* 3 (January 2003), at www.common-place.org; Michael Corcoran, *For Which It Stands: An Anecdotal Biography of the American Flag* (2002); William Rea Furlong and Byron McCandless, *So Proudly We Hail: The History of the United States Flag* (1981); Karal Ann Marling, *Old Glory: Unfurling History* (2004); George Henry Preble, *Origin and History of the American Flag* (1917); Mary Jane Driver Roland, *Old Glory, the True Story* (1918). Also see Thomas H. Pauly, "In Search of the 'Spirit of '76,'" *American Quarterly* 28 (Autumn 1976): 445–64. Robert Justin Goldstein is the authoritative scholar on the history of flag desecration. See his *Saving Old Glory: The History of the American Flag Desecration Controversy* (1995), *Desecrating the American Flag: Key Documents of the Controversy from the Civil War to 1995* (1996), *Burning the Flag: The Great 1989–1990 American Flag Desecration Controversy* (1996), and *Flag Burning and Free Speech: The Case of Texas v. Johnson* (2000). On the flag and American art, see Laurie Adams, *Art on Trial: From Whistler to Rothko* (1976); Albert Boime, "Waving the Red Flag and Reconstituting Old Glory," *Smithsonian Studies in American Art* 4 (1990): 2–25, and *The Unveiling of the Na-*

tional Icons (1998); Steven C. Dubin, *Arresting Images: Impolitic Art and Uncivil Actions* (1992); Michael Kammen, *Visual Shock* (2006); and especially David Rubin, *Old Glory: The American Flag in Contemporary Art* (1994).

Like the first chapter, the final two chapters draw on interviews and coverage provided by local (*Globe, Herald, Phoenix, South Boston Tribune*) and national newspapers (*New York Times, Washington Post, Chicago Tribune*) and magazines (*Time, Newsweek, New Republic, Nation, Harper's, U.S. News and World Report*). On the photographs of 9/11, see David Friend, *Watching the World Change: The Stories Behind the Images of 9/11* (2006). Barry Bluestone and Mary Huff Stevenson, in *The Boston Renaissance: Race, Space, and Economic Change in an American Metropolis* (2000), discuss the demographic shifts in Boston over the past forty years. Susan Orlean, in "Letter from South Boston: The Outsiders," *New Yorker*, July 26, 2004, 44–48, discusses the changes in South Boston. The literature on educational policy and re-segregation is vast. I found especially helpful the reports by Gary Orfield and associates available at www.civilrightsproject.ucla.edu. Also see Charles T. Clotfelter, *After Brown: The Rise and Retreat of School Desegregation* (2004); Jennifer L. Hochschild, *The New American Dilemma: Liberal Democracy and School Desegregation* (1984); John Jackson, *Social Scientists for Social Justice: Making the Case Against Segregation* (2001); Jonathan Kozol, *The Shame of the Nation: The Restoration of Apartheid Schooling in America* (2005); Charles J. Ogletree Jr., *All Deliberate Speed: Reflections on the First Half Century of* Brown v. Board of Education (2004).

Finally, there are several other notable books that make a single photograph their focus: James Bradley and Ron Powers's *Flags of Our Fathers* (2000), Denise Chong's *The Girl in the Picture: The Story of*

Kim Phuc, the Photograph, and the Vietnam War (2000), Paul Hendrickson's *Sons of Mississippi* (2003), and Richard Raskin's *A Child at Gunpoint: A Case Study in the Life of a Photo* (2004). Each work differs from the others in how it analyzes a riveting image and uses it to tell a broader story about Iwo Jima, the Vietnam War, the civil rights movement, and the Holocaust, respectively. But each book focuses on an unforgettable photograph.

INDEX

A NOTE ON THE AUTHOR

LOUIS P. MASUR is William R. Kenan Jr. Professor of American Institutions and Values at Trinity College in Hartford. He is the editor of *Reviews in American History*. His books include *1831: Year of Eclipse* and *Autumn Glory: Baseball's First World Series*.